Play and Development

Play and Development

A Symposium with Contributions by
JEAN PIAGET
PETER H. WOLFF
RENÉ A. SPITZ
KONRAD LORENZ
LOIS BARCLAY MURPHY
ERIK H. ERIKSON

Edited by Maria W. Piers

The Norton Library

W · W · ... New York

Copyright © 1972 by W. W. Norton & Company, Inc.

First published in the Norton Library 1977.

Library of Congress Cataloging in Publication Data
Main entry under title:

Play and development.

Six papers from a series of meetings planned by the
Erikson Institute, the School of Education, and the
Dept. of Psychology of Loyola University, as part of
the university's centennial activities.

Includes bibliographies.

1. Play. 2. Child study. 3. Developmental
psychobiology. I. Piers, Maria W., ed. II. Piaget,
Jean, 1896–   III. Erikson Institute.
IV. Loyola University, Chicago. School of Education.
V. Loyola University, Chicago. Dept. of Psychology.
BF717.P575   155.4'18   72–5261

ISBN 0 393 00871 1

Published simultaneously in Canada
by George J. McLeod Limited, Toronto
PRINTED IN THE UNITED STATES OF AMERICA

*Dedicated to the students
of Erikson Institute for Early Education*

Contents

Preface by Barney Berlin and Robert C. Nicolay 9

JEAN PIAGET   Some Aspects of Operations 15

PETER H. WOLFF   Operational Thought and Social Adaptation 28

RENÉ A. SPITZ   Fundamental Education 43

KONRAD LORENZ   The Enmity between Generations and Its Probable Ethological Causes 64

LOIS BARCLAY MURPHY   Infants' Play and Cognitive Development 119

ERIK H. ERIKSON   Play and Actuality 127

Epilogue by Maria W. Piers 169

Preface

In an age when things are made to wear out quickly and the ephemeral is mistaken for the "relevant," men seek for things that last. It was in this quest that Loyola University of Chicago set forth its centennial celebration. Expressed succinctly in the theme "Knowledge in the Service of Man," this institution in its one hundredth year began a year-long series of symposia, conferences, and meetings to sift out those contributions of the past whose validity has given them a lasting value. As knowledge has replaced mystery with unprecedented speed, contemporary man finds the pursuit of knowledge too often considered as an end in itself. The Loyola University Centennial was one of those rare occasions when vast sectors of man's accumulated knowledge were being examined for the purpose of effecting necessary change.

It was in this context that a series concerning human growth and development was planned. It was envisioned as an attempt at summary and synthesis rather than as an entirely original contribution. Four of the seminal thinkers of the present intellectual world were selected to illuminate their approaches at the border separating knowledge from mystery. The Erikson Institute, School of Education, and Department of Psychology of Loyola University worked together to plan and conduct the series. Each paper in this volume was accompanied by contributions which, although they could not be included, are being gratefully acknowledged. Our thanks go to Prof. Joseph McVickers Hunt of the University of Illinois; Prof. H. J. Rimoldi of Loyola University, Chicago; Dr. Homer Johnson, Professor of Social Psychology, Loyola University, Chicago; Dr. Patricia Barger, Psychology Department and Director of the Child Clinic, Loyola University, Chicago; Dr. Maria Piers, Dean of the Erikson Institute; Dr. Gerhart Piers of the Chicago Institute for Psychoanalysis; Dr. Reginald Lourie of Hillside Hospital, Washington, D.C.; Dr. Evan G. Moore of the Chicago Child Care Society; Prof. Benjamin Blum of the University of Chicago; and Dr. Karl Menninger, The Menninger Foundation, Topeka, Kansas.

The Harris Foundation generously provided us with funds and the Very Reverend James Maguire, S.J., President of Loyola University, together with the Board of Trustees provided the grant to support the series and sponsored accompanying convocations during which honorary doctorates were awarded to participants. The Centennial Anniversary Committee and the Faculty Committee for Centennial Programs gave the original initiative for this series. Mr. John Borgard, Director of the Centennial Programs, provided much of the coordinating and handling of the arrangements. The American College of Surgeons graciously gave the use of their elegant auditorium, and the Chicago Institute for Psychoanalysis, cooperating in many ways, enabled us to move the later scheduled programs to the larger auditorium at the Prudential Building.

Our very special thanks to those who helped to prepare the manuscript for this book: Dr. Paul Weiner from the University of Chicago, Barbara Bowman, Lorraine Wallach, Dr.

Carla Berry, all from the Erikson Institute for Early Education.

While we cannot provide the enviable experience which we had of walking about the Lake Shore Campus of Loyola University in discussions, convocations, ceremonies, and social hours with Jean Piaget, René Spitz, Konrad Lorenz, and Erik Erikson, we hope that this volume will in some way convey the spirit as well as the thought of those occasions. Our greatest wish is that this volume will serve to add to the fulfillment of the centennial theme by placing "Knowledge in the Service of Man."

Barney Berlin and Robert C. Nicolay
Loyola University of Chicago

Play and
Development

JEAN PIAGET

Some Aspects of Operations

In the context of this paper an operation is an action which is internalized and is reversible; that is, it can take place in either direction. It is characteristic for an operation to be part of a total structure. We cannot conceive of a single operation in isolation; rather, each operation is an integral part of a whole, which in turn consists of many operations. For example, the structure of classification consists of many operations of logical classes (grouping of items with common characteristics) or the structure of seriation consists of the operations of putting things into an ascending or descending order. What, then, is a structure? A structure is a system with a set of laws that apply to the system as a whole and not only to its elements. For instance, within the structure of the series of whole numbers there are laws of groups which apply, there are other laws of lattices which apply. Both the laws of group and the laws of lattice apply to the whole system and not just to any isolated number of any isolated element within the system. These laws, moreover, are not static laws, they are laws of transformation. A given structure is characterized by the type of transformation which its laws represent. To give, once again, an example: If, in the series of whole numbers, we add seven plus five, we get twelve. Seven and five are both prime numbers. Twelve, on the other hand, is divisible by two, three, four, and six, so we have, in a real sense, performed a transformation.

A second characteristic of structures is that they are self-regulating; there is a sort of closure. When we apply the laws of transformation to any element of the series of whole numbers, we get another element of the same series. It's a system that is closed in itself and, moreover, we don't have to go outside the system for such laws. The whole system and the functioning of the laws within the system can go on indefinitely without any external elements. An example: A structure is not observable. For this reason many empiricists don't like the notion of structure. They simply don't believe in it. But although it cannot be observed, it is nonetheless a psychological reality. A structure is the sum total of what a child's mind can do. But a child, or indeed an adult, is not aware of the structures that underlie his intellectual work. If an adult knows and applies logic or mathematics, he won't be able to describe to himself the structures that enable him to function intellectually as he does. Even so, the structures exist. As we observe not other people's behavior, but their thought processes, we can see the laws which characterize intellectual structures. Also, we can witness the appearance of new psychological realities when a structure solidifies. For instance, at the moment of solidification, one element brings along the other elements of the structure, so that there is a feeling of intellectual necessity, in fact, inevitability. Let me give you an example:

We have experimented with seriation of sticks of different lengths. We give the child a series of ten sticks differing in about a centimeter in length and ask him to put them in order from the shortest to the longest. Young children respond to this request by putting couples of sticks together: a small one and a big one, a small one and a big one. Some children manage triplets. But that is all they are able to do. Somewhat later on, they will be able to make a real series but they do it by trial and error. They will put down a random number of sticks, and they will correct them until they look right. But eventually, at the age of seven or eight, children go about seriation very systematically. They'll find the smallest stick and then place the smallest of all the sticks that remain next to it; then find the smallest of the remaining ones and place it again until the whole series is constructed. In this way, a child builds his structure without any error and at the same time he is coordinating his actions. One stick, he knows, is bigger than all those that have preceded it, and smaller than all those that remain. He knows this because of the systematic way in which he has built his structure. Here, then, we have the concept of reversibility: If the stick on one end of the series of sticks of unequal lengths is the longest of them all, then the stick on the other end must be the shortest. A seven-year-old learns this all in one action, simpy by virtue of the internal relations involved in the structure.

Now what is this structure? In this instance of seriation which we just mentioned, the structure is a system of asymmetric relationships. We mean by this the following: If stick number one is longer than stick number two, then stick number two cannot possibly be longer than stick number one. The structure is transitive. I would like to look at this aspect of transitivity. If the ability to order things systematically is a real structure, then the child should be capable of carrying out other relationships of transitivity at the same time that he is capable of ordering sticks of different lengths.

We examined this proposition and presented a child with two sticks, stick A being longer than stick B. The child noted which one was longer. Then we hid A, the longer one, under the table and gave the child a third stick, C, which was shorter than the middle-sized one, B, which at this point was clearly visible. We then asked him to compare the two visible sticks with the third hidden one. Young children at the stage where they are making couples in the seriation would say that they couldn't tell whether this one was shorter or longer than the other one, because they hadn't seen them together. But a group of seven- or eight-year-old youngsters, the age when children are able to build seriation systematically, will say, "Well, of course, stick C is shorter than stick A; it just goes without saying."

It is clear, then, that at seven or eight, children experience a feeling of necessity apropos of transitive relationships. They don't have to see the two sticks together; they just know that C must be shorter than A if A is larger than B and B is larger than C. This seems to verify to me the psychological existence of a structure even though structures as such are not observable. What we can observe, however, is a child's behavior in relation to things in his environment, and from this we can infer structure.

My coworkers and I have studied the nature and development of operations for many years. For the past several years, however, we have been working on other problems, of which two experiments in the area of memory shall be discussed here. The first one is based on the above seriation of little sticks of increasing size. In this case, the young children with whom we worked did not construct the order themselves, but were shown a system already made—a system of sticks getting bigger and bigger and bigger. A week later we asked these children what they remembered of it. It turned out that they remembered the experiment in accordance with the stage in which they would have been, had they been asked to construct it themselves. Some of them claimed that a week before we had shown them couples of sticks: a big one, a little one, a big one, a little one, and so on. Others maintained that we had shown them triplets: a big one, a middle-sized one, a small one, a big one, a middle-sized one, a small one, and so on. The striking thing was that the children remembered not what they had perceived, but their own interpretation of the precept. They interpreted the experiment on their own level of assimilation. There is another aspect to this experiment which is even more striking. Six months later, 70 per cent of the same age group of children had a better recollection of what we had shown them than they did a week after the initial demonstration. They had not seen this display in the meantime; instead, we met with them again six months later and asked them if they recalled what we had shown them a long time ago, and 70 per cent of them had progressed in the following manner: Those that had remembered the sticks in couples now remembered triplets.

The memory, then, is a retention of how one has interpreted things at the time of encounter, but it becomes more realistic as the intellectual interpretation improves. Perhaps there is a clue in this for a student preparing for exams. If he starts preparing himself six months before, his memory may have gotten better by the time he has to take the exam.

In another experiment concerning memory, we showed some young children three glass containers, two with water and one empty. Container A had blue water, container B had red water, and C was used as an intermediary so that we could change the red water into glass A and the blue water into glass B. When we questioned these children who had, as yet, no notion of transitivity, as to what they remembered about this little procedure, they didn't recall the use of container C at all. They described what we did in the following manner: "You took this glass (A) and that glass (B) and you poured them into each other, and that changed the red in one of them and the blue in the other." They even started to do it themselves and we had to stop them so that they wouldn't pour their water all over the table. Not being as yet in possession of the structure involved, they totally ignored its existence in this particular experiment. The interesting thing here is that even when we were not interested in operations proper but were looking specifically at memory, we ran into more evidence for the existence of operations. The same happened when we studied the problems of causality. We were, for instance, looking at children's ideas on how movement is transmitted. We had a number of balls in a trough, marked A through H. We let ball A run down the trough to hit the others and all of them stayed still except, of course, for H, which moved off the end of the row. Children who have acquired the notion of transitivity explain this by saying that something moved across this row of little balls from A to H and that it was H where the movement continued. But at an earlier age, they have ideas like this: Ball A came down the trough and then went around behind them and scooted out the other end. So here, when looking at cause-and-effect relations, we run again into the question of the operational level of children. There is, however, one phenomenon of general validity in the development of operations, a phenomenon which I have called decallage: It is the fact that the same operations sometimes appear in the same child at different times, according to the specific content to which they are applied. Thus, children who already have the notion of transitivity of length nonetheless fail to understand the transitivity of weight. We did the following experiment with children who already could solve the problem of transitivity of length: We had two brass cylinders, A and B, of the same size and the same weight. We also had a leaden ball C, which all the children believed to be heavier than either A or B. Then we would ask them to compare B and C on the scale. They would weigh the items and find that C weighed the same as B. That was a big surprise to them, but they believed it. Then we repeated the original question and they would assert again that A and B weighed the same, and that B and C weighed the same. When, however, we asked them, "What about A and C? Aren't they the same weight?" They said, "Oh, no." They wouldn't accept it. "Maybe once (as if by chance) C might weigh the same as A," they conjectured, "but not twice." This sort of thinking goes on until about the age of nine and is analogous to the findings of the Binet-Simon test which consists of ordering five boxes of the same volume but of different weights. That, too, is understood at about nine or ten, but not at an earlier age.

Here is yet another example: According to the law of conservation of matter, the amount of plasticene in a given ball remains constant even if you change its shape. Children of seven or eight years will agree that this is so, but they will not believe until they are nine or ten that two balls weigh the same, even though their shapes differ. The question is *why?* Why do the same operations in the selfsame child occur two or three years apart, if and when they are applied to a different content? The fact is that these operations are concrete. By this we mean that the child understands them only with regard to specific objects. He does not hypothesize, and some objects seem to defy logic more than others. Length, for instance, is a very simple, easily understood characteristic, but not weight. Weight is hard to understand. Young children will say, for instance, that an object dangling from a string high up in the air must be light; and if it hangs down very low, they conclude that it must be heavy.

If one object is resting on another and extends over the edge, they'll say that the part of the object that is resting weighs, but the part that is hanging doesn't weigh. So weight has its own dynamic properties and is much more difficult to put into a logical or operational structure than, say length. A number of authors who criticize my notion of stages forget that there is this quite well documented phenomenon of decallage, which testifies to their existence. One might wonder if it's possible to develop a theory of decallage. I hope so. I think that our work on causality may lead us in that direction. The essential thing, it seems to me, is the nature of the object—the resistance of the object to which the operations are applied.

In the development of operations the subject follows more or less regular laws of development, but not the objects. They vary greatly in being accessible to logic. I would just like to point out that there is a very similar problem in physics, the problem of understanding friction. There is no general theory of friction and each case is explained in its own terms. And the physicist finds it equally as difficult to explain friction as we do explaining decallage.

I would like to turn now to some questions regarding the origin of operations, since they are formed by what I call reflexive abstraction. Simple abstraction leads to finding out properties of objects themselves. If, for instance, we pick up a couple of objects and hold them in our hands and weigh them and find that one is heavier than the other, that is something we have learned about specific objects. It is a qualitative thing about the object. Reflexive abstraction, on the other hand, does not stem from observing objects, but derives from actions—our own actions. I would like to give an example that a friend of mine told me and to which he attributes his career as a mathematician. When he was a small boy, he was counting some stones and he counted them from left to right and found there were ten. Then he counted them from right to left and, lo and behold, there were ten again. Then he put them in a circle, and finding ten once again, he was very, very excited. He found, essentially, that the sum is independent of the order. This is a discovery. It is a reflexive abstraction stemming from his own actions. The order was not in the stones themselves. It was his actions that gave the stones their orderly arrangement. The sum wasn't in the stones either; there was no sum until he came and put the stones in one-to-one correspondence with the number system. What he found, then, was that his action of ordering the stones and his other action of adding them up were independent of one another, and a different ordering action did not lead to a different sum. Reflexive abstraction is a general practice in mathematics. New findings in mathematics are produced by carrying out operations on other operations. Similarly, children develop as they apply psychological operations to other operations. Numerical multiplication, for instance, is simply a series of additions (another kind of operation): Three added to three added to three many times. A further example that develops much later in a child's life is proportionality.* There we have an equality of two relations which themselves depend upon numerical multiplication. And then, even later than that, there is the notion of distributivity, which in turn presupposes the notion of proportions. It's an operation carried out on another operation, namely proportionality. Distributivity may look simple. It may look as if any child who knows how to add and multiply and who understands adding and multiplying could understand the distributive law. But this is not so; distributivity is understood very late in development. We have a couple of experiments in this area, one from the realm of physics. We have an elastic band with some marks on it. We show it to the child and ask him to predict where those marks will be when we stretch the band. Until eleven or twelve years of age, children understand this to be a question of addition. They don't understand that when the elastic is stretched over its whole length, the marks will be distributed differently and that the problem is one of a distributive relationship. They just think that some-

* In a different context, Piaget described an experiment about proportionality involving two kinds of disks, a large number of which—say ten—were marked X and a small number of which—say three—were marked O. The disks were placed in a container and children were asked to reach into the container and to predict how many O disks and X disks they would have picked up.

thing is going to be added somewhere when the elastic is stretched, so they are unable to predict where the marks will be. Some people might point out that what we are talking about is a physical difficulty and not an operational one. To check that, we set up an other experiment. In that one we had two glasses, each about one-third full of water, and another empty glass. We poured the water from the first two into the third one. Then we doubled the amount of water in the third one and asked children to predict where it would be in the first two glasses when we poured it back into them. It is not until eleven or twelve years of age that children are able to predict that there will now be twice as much in glass 1 and 2 because there was twice as much in the third glass. They were able to state that there would be "a little more," but the proportional understanding of distributivity was not at their disposal.

It is the idea of reflexive abstraction which helps us to see development as a series of regulatory thought processes, not only as the necessary result of either heredity or experience. I have two colleagues on whom I've been calling in my work, one of them named Berlin, who is a neobehaviorist and sees me as a neobehaviorist also. The other one, named Belling, is a maturationist and sees me as a maturationist also. To Berlin, then, intellectual knowledge comes from contacts with the external world, whereas Belling thinks that it is all a question of maturation of the nervous system. The truth is that I am neither a maturationist nor a neobehaviorist. I am an interactionist. What interests me is the creation of new thoughts that are not preformed, not predetermined by nervous system maturation nor predetermined by encounters with the environment, but are constructed within the individual himself, constructed internally through the process of reflexive abstraction and constructed externally through the process of experience. There is, in other words, a third hypothesis possible, in addition to the behaviorist's and the maturationist's. It is not maturation per se or the environment in and of itself which brings about intellectual development. Rather, it is education which makes reflexive abstraction possible. This goes for intellectual processes in general and in particular for language. Language has a logic of its own and implicit operations.

I would like, at this juncture, to describe some experimental work which was done by Hermine St. Clair in our laboratories in Geneva. She took two groups of children, one of "conservers" (children who understand the principle of conservation of a given volume or weight) and the other of "nonconservers." She found that there were significant systematic differences in the way they used language in certain areas. For instance, the "nonconservers" used what linguists call scalers. They would describe things in terms of being big and little and fat. Whereas the "conservers" used what linguists call vectors or comparatives; for instance, "this pencil is bigger than that one, but it's thinner than," and so on. So there clearly was here a demonstrable and tight connection between linguistic level and operational level. Then she went on to do some work with the first group, the "nonconservers," to train them to use language that was similar to the language of the "conservers." She trained them in the use of comparatives and the other characteristics of the more highly developed language, thinking that perhaps the more sophisticated language would lead to a higher level of operational thinking in these children. When she retested them, however, she found that they used the more sophisticated language but there was almost no difference in their operational thinking. Words did not change their thought processes, although 10 per cent of them did make a small cognitive progress with the help of vocabulary. These children, however, were probably in an interstage and ready for the next cognitive step anyway. Language, then, does not seem to be the way to develop intelligence in children.

By way of concluding, I would like to speak a few words on the pedagogical applications of what I've been telling you today. I'm not an educator, I have no advice to give. Education is an area of its own and educators must find the appropriate methods, but what I've found in my research seems to me to speak in favor of an active methodology in teaching. Children should be able to do their own experimenting and their own research. Teachers, of course, can guide them by providing appropriate materials, but the essential thing is that in order for a child to understand something, he must construct it himself, he must re-invent it. Every time we teach a child something, we keep him from inventing it himself. On the other hand, that which we allow him to discover by himself will remain with him visibly, as it did in the case of my mathematician friend, for all the rest of his life.

PETER H. WOLFF

Operational Thought and Social Adaptation

One of the concerns of education, here and now, is specifically the education of disadvantaged children so as to help them to acquire the necessary intellectual competence to compete adequately in our industrial society. Since the Pandora's box of the United States class structure was opened and the plight of the poor was finally accepted as a reality, and it became apparent that equal opportunity of education was a cruel hoax, educational psychologists have tried various means of correcting the great intellectual and educational deficits from which such a large segment of Americans suffer. As each aspirant treatment for the disease of poverty and inequality has failed, there has been a tendency to look earlier and earlier for interventions which would correct the unfortunate situation. Yet solutions do not come easily. Some individuals have proposed that only a social revolution and a total reconstruction of society would be effective therapy. With a considerable amount of justification they regard the problem as being not primarily one that can be treated by improved psychological technology. Others have stressed the need for earlier and more vigorous psychological enrichment as the treatment of choice without making clear what riches would be needed to benefit the disadvantaged, and without demonstrating that such enrichment procedures in themselves have had any significant effect to date. It is therefore only natural that we would look to the studies from the Geneva group in the hope of extracting practical lessons for the education and re-education of disadvantaged populations of children. Piaget's discoveries have had an extensive, even though only superficial, influence on the climate of American psychology and even on the curriculum in elementary and high schools. This effect has been felt mostly in the upper-middle-class school system, where the approach to the teaching of mathematics, geometry, and physics has been radically altered by the insight into the intellectual growth of children given us by Piaget and his coworkers. Healthy as this influence is in its own right, it has really not touched the real problem facing us in the education of children from the American rural and urban ghettos. Furthermore, Piaget has expressed justifiable skepticism about the premature application of his discoveries as a technical manual for education, perhaps because he feared that we would fall into the old army edict: "Do something; do it even if it's wrong."

The crisis facing American education is not so much the lack of increasingly clear methods for obtaining information about how poor learners can learn as that we really don't know how children acquire the fundamental operations of logical thought—children, that is, who start life at high risk and spend their early years in a grossly distorted environment as it is reflected in their homes, their neighborhoods, their schools, and their society, which provide them neither with stable representations of the real world nor intrinsic motivations to structure its universal properties. We are by now all familiar with the currently popular methods of psychological engineering as they have been applied to children; and I will not dwell here on the pros and cons of these efforts to accelerate intellectual development by environmental enrichment, by techniques based on the proposition that almost anything can be taught to any child at any age as long as it is presented rationally. Whether or not it is possible to effect quantitative shifts in rates of cognitive acquisition by massive enrichment programs which without such problems would proceed at a more leisurely pace is itself not of great theoretical interest. There seems little reason to doubt that a grossly distorted environment will delay the acquisition of logical structures, and there is some reason to assume that such carefully programmed enrichment procedures might within narrow limits accelerate the rate of intellectual development in retarded children, even though the evidence to date is not persuasive. Whether or not the latter is a desirable goal, if it is at all possible, I leave to your judgment since it is not a question on which Piaget's formulations and evidence would shed much light.

A theoretically more interesting question, however, is the possibility that gross disturbances in the acquisition devices for intelligence due to organic pathology or gross environmental distortion of the type encountered in rural and urban ghettos will result not only in quantitative shifts but also in qualitative distortions of the sequence or form of intellectual structures. Or inversely, that environmental manipulation can modify these distortions. The most extreme distortions of this type would be actual stage reversals, and all the evidence to date of which I am aware indicates that no significant reversals occur in the stages of cognitive development (see, for example, Gouin-Decarie 1965; and Pinard and Laurendeaux 1964).

A less extreme qualitative shift in the development of intellectual functions would be revealed if we were to discover that children reared under such pathological circumstances can devise alternative pathways to the same end point, end point here being defined as the major stages of development (stable structures of the whole). The question would, in other words, be of interest if we were to discover that the sequences which have been described as being natural or "optimal" are only one among a set of possible sequences, and that alternative pathways similar to what Heinz Werner has called analogous processes come to the foreground under grossly modified environmental circumstances.

In a third kind of variation, the one perhaps most commonly encountered, the child simply does not progress beyond a certain upper limit (probably somewhere in the range of the concrete operations) or else he makes brief advances into the realm of formal operations but then regresses to a lower level of concrete thought. (Our current political spectacle and military fiasco suggests that a significant proportion of the adult population which is considered to be normal and is often in positions of great power appears to function at a level well below that of formal operations. There is a substantive question whether even in an advanced industrial society, a significant proportion of the population does indeed operate at a level of cognitive formal thought consistently higher than that which we are generally inclined to associate with economic poverty and social discrimination. This, however, is again not a matter of direct concern to us today.) The second possibility—namely that there may be alternative pathways toward the establishment of overall logical structures of the whole—should be a matter of direct interest to educators, since it would crystallize our task as doing detailed investigations of individual differences in the strategies of cognitive development in order to discover which among the alternative pathways for intellectual development are "most natural," which ones are most consistent with the environment in which disadvantaged children develop, and the like. Thus, different children may come to the same logical structures by varying pathways depending on the experience in their disordered world as well as depending on organic pathology and cultural expectation. The question of alternative pathways or analogous processes (Werner 1957) is also a critical question in psychology which has insufficiently occupied investigators to date, and it goes beyond the issue of individual differences.

Furth (1966) has carried out systematic studies on deaf children to indicate that the capacity to speak is not a prerequisite for logical differentiation; Lenneberg's studies of children who never spoke because of neurological deficits provided clinical evidence that highly differentiated logical thought may proceed without the acquisition of spoken language. Piaget has also brought persuasive arguments to indicate that although language and thought are mutually interdependent, they are not identical expressions of one unitary structure, and that the early development of symbolic thought does proceed independent of the acquisition of language. It is as conceivable that concrete operations might develop, become differentiated, and even hypertrophy independently of acquisition. Such discrepancies between thought and language development would in the long run probably set an upper ceiling on the extent to which a child will advance.

For theoretical purposes we may consider an extreme hypothetical example of a child born with severe cerebral palsy, which has affected primarily his sensory and motor cortex but has left the association areas and sensory integration areas intact. While such a child would be unable to carry out any sensorimotor transactions on the objects in his environment, it is likely that he would achieve a preoperational and probably an operational level of symbolic intelligence even though at a somewhat later age than his normal peers. How does such a hypothetical child pass from the simple sensorimotor interactions to the level of symbolic thought? Are the displacements of objects perceived by moving his eyes surfaceably enough to establish object permanence and the reversibility or displacement in space which are so necessary for the interiorization of logical structures? Or does a child under such extreme pathological conditions make use of alternative modes by structuring the constants of his environment and thereby elaborate the corresponding thought operation? In a set of closely watched twins who were unable to stand, crawl, or walk at two years of age and had great difficulty in hand-eye coordination, we found that as they improved through appropriate rehabilitation in the hospital, they also began to make what we considered their first efforts to displace themselves in space. Both twins, however, learned to walk in a fashion that was unlike any kind of walking or crawling I had observed in other children. They crawled by keeping their knees almost extended although they had contractures of the hamstring muscles which made this kind of crawling more difficult than the usual type, and by this device they eventually began to walk. The same twins developed other aberrant sequences in motor development which only eventually resulted in the developmental milestones which are generally held to be normative. Due to their pathological early environmental experiences, these children seem thus to have devised unique alternative developmental pathways toward a final common goal which could not be considered simply as delays in development but seem to represent analogous processes as a means to the end point of walking. The questions which these observations raised for me was whether the development we are inclined to consider as normative and which Piaget has described in such exquisite detail is not one of a number of alternative developmental sequences, although it is the one most commonly observed under natural circumstances, whereas the alternative processes are activated only when the environment blocks the developmental pathways and forces the child to devise what might be considered aberrant direction. This proposition would be analogous to what one knows to be the case in biochemistry where an alternative metabolic path is put into action when a particular sequence is blocked. Thus the nervous system of the twins in question might have had at its disposal alternative pathways for motor development which are never apparent in normal situations but were called into action because of very deviant environmental circumstances. This is the case in biochemical processes, and if it is possibly the case in motor development, why could it not also apply to intellectual development? We might then ask more generally what happens when the usual developmental path is blocked as in the case of extreme environmental deprivation, organic pathology, or the like and might raise the possibility that the organism discovers (somewhat) unique solutions although they will converge on the final goals of operational structures of the kind so persuasively described by Piaget as representing the most nearly stable adaptive relations between the intellect and the physical world. Werner's studies of analogous cognitive processes in children and Goldstein's investigations of brain-injured adults provide indirect evidence that such alternative pathways or safety factors may indeed be built into the functional organization of the nervous system. The task of developmental psychology especially in its practical applications to educational methods must then consider strategies which will not force all children into the same "normative" route as represented in the current school system, even as represented in a more sophisticated and enlightened theory of education, but instead to determine the range of alternative means to the same goal.

Piaget's theories are based on the discovery that thought is the interiorization of sensorimotor interactions with the environment and that the transition from sensorimotor to thought operation represents a universal direction of individual development. This formulation has given rise to a number of misunderstandings about the essential nature of sensorimotor action for cognitive development for which we can hardly blame Piaget or anyone else from the Geneva group. To some it has suggested that in view of the unidirectionality of development, it should be possible to correct deficits in cognitive development by training intellectually retarded children in perceptual motor tasks. Thus major systems of rehabilitation make it a common practice to put children with learning deficits through their paces by encouraging them to engage in rote repetition, copying designs, jumping, bouncing, crawling, or being "patterned" through repetitive movements of the limbs, in the hope that such busy work will correct the cognitive defect. The misconception finally resides in the notion that children who have missed something at one stage of development can only improve themselves if they make up this deficit at a subsequent stage in development, as if motor training of the child at six and seven was the equivalent of motor exercise of the two- and three-year-old child and therefore would have a direct bearing on the correction of his cognitive defects. Far more rational would seem to be those attempts which seek to discover how children with learning difficulties are deficient in their cognitive operations in a manner appropriate to their level of differentiation and would then devise the various alternative processes by which the children could master those dimensions in which they are defective. The obligation of developmental and educational research must therefore divert its focus from the hope that one can improve cognition by magical procedures of having children crawl up and down ladders. The demonstration of multilinear means toward a common goal as well as the acceptance of the existence of different final goals in intellectual development would be essential aspects of a rational approach to the corrective education of children to whom the Erikson Institute is devoting such great efforts and care.

A number of years ago David Rapaport brought to our attention the need for a mathematization of clinical theory of psychoanalysis in order to take it out of its current amorphous intuitive framework. Clearly he was not pleading for a witless quantification of data that besets the bulk of American psychology but was making a suggestion that the knowledge which had been gathered through clinical theory of psychoanalysis or personality development could come into being (Rapaport 1960; see also George Klein 1969).

The development of logical operations has raised for me the additional question whether the concept in its most general form, although it was specifically formulated to codify man's systematic acquisition of knowledge about the physical world, might nevertheless also have applications in other dimensions of psychological development, specifically in personality development of the kind with which psychoanalytic theory has been most occupied. Specifically the possibility occurred to me that one might be able to formalize the characteristics of interpersonal transactions—for example, characterize what are the general properties of interchange between infant and parent, between peer and peer, between child and society—since these are the primary concerns of clinicians working with individuals and their emotional development. Operations are most generally defined by Piaget as interiorized actions. By this he means, for example, that the mental operations of addition and subtraction are the interiorized representations of actual manipulations of concrete objects. Such a specific definition, however, does not do justice to the power of the concept within the framework of the theory of sensorimotor development and genetic epistemology since it does not convey the full significance of what this concept must do within the theory. It ignores, for example, the parallel concepts of reversibility, equilibration, the structuration of the whole, and the concept of logical operation. It is unlikely that anything comparable to the combinatorial logic used by Piaget to rationalize the ontogenesis of logical thought with its associated concepts of reversibility and equilibration can be directly transposed when we attempt to formalize the affective development of children. If anything, such a formal system is most clearly implied in Erikson's psychosocial formulations of personality development, but even here the formal definition of stages is hardly separated from their contents, so that in their present formulation the concepts of mode, modality, and Erikson's conception of epigenesis do not yet lend themselves to a mathematization of interpersonal relationships.

In another context Piaget has proposed that the concept of will might serve as an affective operation whose overall function in development parallels that of biological operations in cognitive development. Thus he proposed that the regulation of isolated desires in terms of stable systems of values (adapted to the norms of the society) and the subordination of momentary desire to consideration to past and future conduct within a rational system of values requires an effort of will and in this sense the concept might serve as an affective operation which will relate the parts to the whole. More generally Piaget has insisted throughout his writings that intellectual and social affective development of children are inseparable aspects of one unitary process although he emphasizes that there is no homogeneous structure which will adequately cover the development of intellectual and affective behavior (WHO publication, 1963). Thus he proposes that at the level of sensory motor functions a lack of differentiation between inside and outside, or action and object, is paralleled by a stage of primary narcissism in the child's affective life since at that point in his development he has no perspective on the needs of others or of independent causal properties residing in others. As the sensorimotor phase of development comes to a close and the child gains some awareness of objects as entities independent of his action, there is also the beginning of a tie to the social partner—in other words, the beginning of an object relationship with a full awareness of the other as something separate from himself which is marked by recognition of what is familiar, what is a stranger, and a fear of the loss of the familiar. Such effective decentering runs parallel to the cognitive decentering described in such detail in Piaget's descriptions of early sensorimotor development; again the two are assumed to be interdependent functionally but not to share a common structure. With the acquisition of concrete thought operations, Piaget finds parallel transitions in the child's affective life as he becomes aware of duty as a concept and as this awareness in turn leads him to subordinate his own wishes to the expectations of mutual respect and reciprocity. The child is now able to consider other points of view in the social and affective sphere as well as in the cognitive realm. With the onset of formal operations, the adolescent elaborates large value systems which have stability over time and within which momentary desires must always be subordinated to the awareness of abstract values.

Piaget's formulation is admittedly incomplete, and the parallels between the cognitive and affective development as he has suggested them pertain primarily to the individual's relationship to his society, his normative values, and at best his concepts of morality. Thus they do not pertain to what individuals actually do in everyday life so much as they pertain to what human beings think about in moments of reflection and rational thought. In order to describe what people actually do at various stages of their development, one might, however, employ the concept of operations in a more specific way in order to distinguish, for example, between the child's relation to his mother and the mother's relationship to her child. Surely this is not a transitive or reciprocal relationship. Similarly we might attempt to formalize the distinction between the relation of school-age peers and the relation of a younger child to an older child. Further, we might distinguish between the relation of man to wife and wife to man, even though the women's liberation movement might insist that there are no differences. In other words, we would have to empirically investigate what are the universal properties of such relationships, which ones are transitive or intransitive, which ones are reflexive, which ones are symmetrical, and from this crude analysis we might arrive at a system of relationships which define the growing child's everyday transactions with his environment.

In a more refined way, Piaget has studied the problem of logical relations and elaborated them into "structures of the whole" for entirely different purposes (classes, numbers, and relations). These efforts, however, pertain primarily to logical understanding and not to social action so that our application as it is proposed here could not hope to approach the degree of distinction between form and content that Piaget was able to achieve in his description of the logical relation. This is the problem we encounter when we attempt to extract from Erikson's formulations for psychosocial development more formal structures; it is apparent when we make such an effort that the concept of the mode is defined very much by its content and that its formal or vectorial properties alone do not lend themselves to being integrated into a system of formal properties inherent in psychological development. Furthermore, we may entertain the possibility that psychopathology may one day be definable in terms of such formal relations—namely the failure to distinguish between transitive and intransitive relationships in everyday transactions; we may be able to describe in universal terms, for example, the father who treats his child as if he were a pal, who neglects the fact that the child is a child and the father an adult, and thus defines the formal aspect of this properly intransitive relationship and it now becomes distorted under the guise of a pseudo equality or pseudo reciprocity.

In the most speculative manner I therefore have wondered whether the concept of operation if it were translated into actual transactions between individuals and then abstracted into their formal properties might become a useful language for describing the social development of children with respect to their parents, peers, younger children, and for describing simultaneously the development of the parents with respect to their children. No isolated description would do any more than translate what is clinically known into different terms, but once the total system of interactions into any individual were collected into a system of formal terms, one might begin to describe the varieties and levels of interactions in their formal terms that are available to any individual.

I am reminded of an event that occurred while we were observing the delivery of an infant by a Japanese woman who was attended by her obstetrician without the benefit of anesthesia. During the first stage of labor she and her obstetrician conversed in the usual polite mode of address, the woman talking to the doctor in the respectful form, the doctor addressing the woman in the polite but less honorific mode. By the end of the second and the beginning of the third stage of labor the patient had become so absorbed in her activity that her language changed and she now resorted to a form used only by children when addressing their mothers. The obstetrician responded in kind, speaking to her as if he were indeed her parent, and similarly dropped the polite form. At the end of the labor both the patient and the doctor returned to their formal modes of address. What the Japanese language has codified in its highly inflected modes of address illustrates, I believe, what we should mean by speaking of formal operations and the actual relations between individuals. Such an approach would force us to return to the phenomenology of of relationship without the highly convoluted theoretical structures based on the flow of energies from one person to another; it might also help us to make a rational theory of personality development into a systematic developmental theory.

BIBLIOGRAPHY

Furth, H. G. *Thinking without Language: Psychological Implications of Deafness.* New York: Free Press, 1966.

Gouin-Decarie, T. *Intelligence and Affectivity in Early Childhood.* New York: International Universities Press, 1965.

Klein, G. S. "Freud's Two Theories of Sexuality." In *Clinical-Cognitive Psychology*, edited by L. Berger, pp. 136–81. Englewood Cliffs, N.J.: Prentice-Hall, 1969.

Piaget, J. "The General Problems of the Psychobiological Development of the Child." In *Discussions of Child Development IV*, edited by J. M. Tanner and B. Inhelder, pp. 3–23. New York: International Universities Press, 1960.

Pinard, A., and Laurendeaux, M. *Causal Thinking in Children.* New York: International Universities Press, 1964.

Rapaport, D. "Psychoanalysis as a Developmental Psychology." In *Perspectives in Psychological Theory: Essays in Honor of Heinz Werner*, edited by B. Kaplan and S. Wapner, pp. 209–55. New York: International Universities Press, 1960.

Werner, H. *The Comparative Psychology of Mental Development*, rev. ed. New York: International Universities Press, 1957.

RENÉ A. SPITZ

Fundamental Education

The Coherent Object as a Developmental Model

What is fundamental education?

Education—without the qualifying word *fundamental*—is variously defined as "bringing up the young" (Oxford Dictionary, also Webster) or "a preparation for complete living" (H. Spencer 1861), "the science and art of human development" (Baldwin 1940). It is worthwhile to remember that the original meaning of the word *Education* is "to lead out of."

For the purpose of the present study, I will use a recent definition which states that Education is the process of producing change in the individual (John T. Goodlad, UCLA). The term *Learning*, on the other hand, will be reserved for input and storage of information in our memory banks.

To our mind Education and Learning differ radically from each other, both developmentally and structurally.

From the developmental viewpoint Education is probably

the more archaic process of the two and the capacity of the individual to be changed by Education is probably inborn. Education always involves a change of the id, therefore it largely takes place in the unconscious. Education also lays the foundation for the body ego (the way one experiences one's body) and the capacity for object relations. As the human being becomes more differentiated, Education becomes increasingly based on identification and other defense mechanisms and leads to a change of the whole self, and often to a change of the ego as well. In other words, Education may also shape our skills and coping devices, even though we are usually not aware of it.

Learning, on the other hand, is largely a conscious process. It too changes our self, but frequently does so without the intervention of the id. Moreover, Learning leaves impermanent memory traces, which, but for periodic reinforcement, would deteriorate and eventually disappear. Yet Education is an indispensable prerequisite for Learning.

A rather striking example of the difference between Education and Learning could be observed in the history of the baby's toilet training in our country in the thirties. At that time the Children's Bureau recommended the beginning of toilet training already in the second month of life. The babies actually learned, when placed on the potty, to do their duty. But at the end of the first year the training broke down. At that time it came into conflict with the child's developing personality, specifically with his need to assert his own free will. Under these circumstances, the reinforcement of mere Learning was not strong enough to prevent the breakdown, which, incidentally, proved to be exceedingly difficult to overcome.

Toilet training based on Education begins much later, namely, during the second year of life. By then the ego has become operative. The child has a sense of self, he registers his bodily sensations and on the basis of affective reciprocity identifies with his mother's wishes and incorporates her standards. Ferenzci called this process the Establishment of Sphincter Morality. It is the first occasion on which the child internalizes the "thou shalt not . . . ," a first installment of the decalogue as it were. This lesson will last. It is acquired by Education, not by Learning, and will remain operative throughout life. The example of toilet training and the two ways of achieving it illustrates the essential question of this paper: What constitutes Fundamental Education, as opposed to Learning, and when does it begin? I have postulated elsewhere that the process which produces change in the child is brought about through an affective interchange with the mother or mother substitute. Accordingly it begins at birth, and because of the helplessness of young human beings, it continues throughout the first few years of life. Education, in leading the child out of a state of dependence, is, then, among other things a means to insure the child's survival. It brings the newborn from an unconscious and undifferentiated state to greater differentiation and conscious mentation and to the body ego (muscular coordination and goal directed actions). The latter constitutes the beginning of the ego, that central steering organization of the psyche which makes all mastery of the outer world and the inner world possible. Affective interchange begins in the very first hour of life and since all later development is predicated on it, I have called it Fundamental Education. Without it a complete arrest in development occurs and the infant's survival is in jeopardy. This I have shown twenty-five years ago in my studies on emotionally deprived so-called Hospitalism Children.

Fundamental Education goes from random activity at birth, via interaction with the surround (of which the mother simply appears a part and which is ensured by innate S-R behavior), to interaction with the mother seen as an adult partner, to imitation of her, and then to identification with her. The last two, of course, can be observed in any parent-child relationship. Let me illustrate imitation and identification with one example:

A little boy, Tommy, fifteen to eighteen months old, had been taken by his mother to a seashore resort, where his father visited them on weekends. After the first visit, when father had left, the little boy took one of father's huge hats and one of his walking canes and with the hat engulfing his head and trying to swing the cane, he marched up and down the room uttering in a deep growl, "Daddy, Daddy." The little boy is manifestly playing "Daddy" but without the least idea of *what* "Daddy" means; this is an imitation of daddy's gestures.

Identification proper, which begins to develop at a somewhat later period, is a far more complex process. But at the time when the imitative precursor of identification begins, we can also witness the first beginnings of thought processes.

But if it be true that thinking can only begin as the outcome of parent-child relations, then we must ask ourselves what happens if the child is deprived of them?

In cases of complete deprivation neither speech nor thinking processes are acquired. The child communicates only by his physical actions, that is, fight or flight. The humanization of man is arrested; the domestication of the drives is jeopar-

dized. In view of the role and nature of Fundamental Education, I am inclined to look with misgivings on the claims made
for the so-called advanced learning devices, the teaching ma-
chines and computers. They may bring about rapid results, but
I doubt the permanence of these results. Moreover, no teaching machine would ever have induced little Tommy to imitate
his father, hat, walk, voice, and all. For the imitation sprang
from Tommy's admiration and his desire to be like father.
Had he admired a computer instead, he might have ended up
clicking and whirring—and lost father's contribution to his
humanization. Humanization can only occur via affect-charged
interchange for which, luckily, there are countless opportunities for a father and his son.

In children who don't have the chance to admire adults and
identify with them, the ability for concept formation and
word symbols is either absent or gravely impaired. Since the
time when I first described Hospitalism, research in infancy
has continued in several directions. The ones discussed here
concern the following developmental achievements: sleep,
smile, early perception, and finally object and object constancy.

The following concerns *sleep*.

At the Medical Center of the University of Colorado a team
of young researchers, with whom I am associated as consultant,
have been conducting for a number of years an extensive
series of investigations under the leadership of Dr. Robert
Emde * and Dr. David Metcalf.† They are studying the spe-

* Dr. Emde, Associate Professor, Department of Psychiatry, University of
Colorado School of Medicine, Denver, Colorado.
† Dr. Metcalf, Associate Professor, Department of Psychiatry, University
of Colorado School of Medicine, Denver, Colorado, and Director of the
Division of Electroencephalography and EEG Research.

cific details of those patterns in Fundamental Education and Learning which in the course of my previous research I was unable to explore, because neither the more sophisticated application of the EEG nor the investigation of sleep patterns and REM were available at the time.

One of these patterns is that of neonatal sleep. Emde and his team verified some of the predictions I made: that newborn sleep is basically different from sleep at any later age, be that preschool child or adult. I based this thesis partly on direct observation of sleeping newborns. But I also reasoned that the term *sleep* in our sense becomes meaningless before the child is born.

As yet we do not know whether there is anything comparable to sleep *in utero*. Does the fetus have a motility pattern? A REM cycle? What is the pattern of its EEG? Do the patterns follow a circadian rhythm?

As of now we are only justified in speaking of sleep or rather of its precursor during the first twenty-four hours of life. That is where Drs. Emde and Metcalf and their collaborators started new investigations. It was based on direct behavioral observations, of sleep-wakefulness patterns, of drowsy- and sleep-REM patterns with simultaneous EEG tracings. This investigation showed a dramatic and relatively rapid development from the newborn's twilight state to a pattern of alternating sleep and wakefulness. Like everything else in nature, sleep, then, does not come ready-made, but changes with maturation. In connection with this I should mention that in a series of twenty-four-hour observations, Dr. Louis Sanders of Boston University was able to pinpoint the change over from the neonatal sleep pattern to a diurnal one. He also demonstrated that conditions which influenced the mother-child relationship would result in a changed sleep rhythm even in the first two months after the baby's birth.

Here we have, I believe, the very first result of Fundamental Education: a behavior originally governed exclusively by neurophysiological and hormonal processes has now been altered by affective mother-child interaction. In principle then, the newborn infant learns to sleep from his mother. Conversely the infant deprived of mothering develops severe disturbances in his sleep-wakefulness patterns, disturbances which can take the form of insomnia or its counterpart, lethargy.

Another behavior pattern which the Emde team investigated was the inception and unfolding of *The Smiling Response* (Polak, Emde, and Spitz 1964). Based on previous research, among which my own (Spitz 1946), they demonstrated with the help of more sophisticated research methods successive stages in the acquisition of the smile.

At birth endogenous smiling can be observed. It is a spontaneous tension discharge and is triggered from inside. In the course of the first trimester the infant's smiling is, however, triggered by outside stimuli and becomes a message to the outside world.

Sleep, by contrast is triggered from inside. It is a regressive process with the function of re-establishing the stimulus barrier by a withdrawal from the outside world (Spitz 1965).

The specific outside stimulus for the infant's smile is the mother's face, or rather the sign Gestalt of that face. It is a potent evocatory stimulus. So is the infant's smile, but in the opposite direction. It evokes the mother's wish to caress the baby and to have his body touch hers. The baby's smile is so compelling that Wayne Dennis and his wife, performing the experiment of raising an infant without smiling at him, found the task insurmountably difficult. The infant's smile, then, becomes the starting point for all later social relations and the paradigm for reciprocal, affective mother-child relations. My earliest document of endogenous smiling is a film taken on the third day of life. Dr. Emde's team has filmed even earlier smiles. As stated before, the neuromuscular pattern of smiling is present at birth but the subsequent development of the smile is indeed linked to the mother's ministration. Without it the baby's endogenous smile never changes and eventually amounts to the idiot's smile (Provence and Lipton 1962), as can be seen in one of my films taken of an eight-month-old completely deprived of maternal care.

In a normal child the smile undergoes the following developmental stages. At about six weeks the infant smiles in response to any outside stimulus. It should be stressed that this new behavior is accompanied by a specific change in the EEG. At about twelve weeks the infant smile can be evoked reliably by a human face. Also, as I demonstrated, by a cardboard mask. Also by a life-sized colored photograph (P. Polak). For what elicits the smile at this juncture is the sight of the hairline, the nose, and two eyes, provided they are in motion. One step further and the two-dimensional representation is not accepted anymore. The infant then smiles only at a *three-dimensional visual stimulus*.

In other words, the infant has now turned from inside perception to outside perception and with it goes a dramatic modification of brainwave patterns (Emde and Metcalf 1969). How does the perception of the environment come about, and what are its accompanying phenomena?

I submit that in the first six months of life and perhaps even later, percepts of one and the same object, mediated by our five senses or rather by their sensory receptors, are perceived as separate unconnected stimuli and laid down as separate memory traces without being fused into a syncretic totality percept. Therefore, a thing touched by the hand, a "touch-toy," will be remembered differently from one heard, a "noise-toy," or from one tasted or seen.

It is hardly possible for the adult to imagine such an absence of coherence between the mnemic traces originating from various percepts provoked by *one single* object. For the adult, the *mention* of an object (or its memory) recreates a complex coherent image. For instance, the word *apple* (particularly if we happen to be hungry), brings back the feel of its hard, crunchy juiciness between our teeth, its tart and sweet taste, its pervasive perfume with a hint of bitter almonds, while we visualize its shiny, red roundness. Memory goes even further: One is easily able to remember a particular apple which one ate twenty years ago.

But when one tires to re-experience the taste of a medicine tasted just once, before the age of two, he probably finds a number of attributes missing. He may remember its color but not the shape of the bottle; not why he hated or loved it. Perhaps its cloying taste, but not its smell. These gaps in the evoked memory are a consequence of the fact that the medicine had not yet become a coherent object representation. And this gives us an inkling of what the perceptual world of the infant is like.

In the newborn, touch and taste are completely separate from the visual picture. He recognizes the feeling of the nipple in his mouth and responds specifically to it. Perhaps, after a while, he recognizes the taste of the milk. He experiences these quasi-separate objects five times a day, at least for half an hour.

Yet during the first four to six months he cannot connect the image of the milk bottle with the taste of milk.

Only later on will he be able to connect and integrate into one coherent object the discrete memory traces of vision, smell, and touch. Among those three there is a leading sensory receptor: vision. As has been proved repeatedly both by observation and experiment, that visual perception is the modality which mediates between the first memory traces. At that age, between six and twelve weeks, the infant recognizes the sign Gestalt of the need-gratifying object (Spitz and K. M. Wolf 1946). In view of these facts I am proposing a somewhat modified model of object relations. Before doing so, I would like to define two terms, the *ego* and the *ego nuclei*.

The ego, in psychoanalytic theory, is the central steering and adaptive organization of the personality. As such it connects motility with perception and volition, it mediates between the demands of reality and the needs and desires coming from the inside. Some of these inside needs stem from the drives (id), others from the conscience (superego). During the first two or three months no ego can be observed, but thereafter it begins to function, regulating drive discharge for the purpose of adaptation. Although the ego per se is not inborn, we postulate that some of its elements are. Edward Glover called these inborn elements Ego Nuclei.

They can be detected even at birth. One such nucleus serves food intake and is therefore contained in the oral cavity, the perioral region (mouth), the stomach, the hand, the middle ear, and the skin surface. In other words, this ego nucleus is contained in all the organs which later on will serve food intake.

During the first weeks certain adaptive patterns related to eating begin to cluster around this ego nucleus. At the same time hunting for the nipple becomes briefer and more goal directed. From here on we may pose the following hypotheses:

The infant remembers the mother's face-in-motion, and there is a secondary clustering of memory traces—supplied by senses other than vision, for instance, hearing, touching, smelling—around the image of the mother's face, consisting of elements which fill in details (nose, mouth, etc.) and accessory details to the same face. Toward the eighth week of life these elements are being fused and structured, and a coherent representation of the mother emerges in the child's mind. During the following six months (age eight to ten months) the details become more precise and the relationship between mother and child is being elaborated. Thereafter the mother becomes a libidinal object, and in due time achieves object constancy (the infant now insists that the same mother ministrate to his needs).

To summarize: Separate percepts, stimulated by the mother's care, are being associated with each other and eventually form a coherent object, with whom the infant then continually interacts and whom he wants near him above everyone else.

This hypothesis has various advantages. Firstly, it offers us a better understanding of the synthetic function of the ego: the rapidly increasing affective interchange between mother and child forms the connection between memory traces of the mother's face and the ego nucleus (the sensation in and around the mouth), resulting eventually in a full-fledged ego.

Secondly, the hypothesis suggests the existence of a transitional phase between an organic (embryological) synthetic function and the psychological synthetic function (or synthetic function of the ego).

At this point we are dealing with the oral stage. The oral

ego nucleus has so many functions that, even at birth, its privileged role for future ego formation is insured. This is so because the oral cavity (mouth) contains three of the five sensory organs, namely those for tactile, gustatory, and olfactory perception (Spitz: Primal Cavity). It is not without interest that perception through these three organs is extensive, vague, and diffuse. It is what Werner (developmental psychology) calls syncretic. In contradistinction the perception of human beings older than twelve months is conscious, intensive, and localized, or, as Werner calls it, diacritic.

It now becomes necessary that we explore the role of vision in the structuring of the psyche. Vision categorically differs from the previously mentioned three sensory modalities—taste, smell, and touch—for vision is invariably diacritic. Vision introduces into the infant's world, in which so far contact perception predominated, the new and fateful distance perception. Because of distance perception the child begins to understand continuity in time and coherence in space. Vision thus establishes a time-span continuum in the mind. It thereby assumes the leadership in the progressive adaptation to the environment and makes a coherent object representation possible. For only now that the child can see, does he realize that the mother who is coming closer and closer and finally picks him up is indeed the same person who walks away, who seems to become smaller and smaller, and ultimately vanishes through a door. As he remembers his mother, coming and going, the feel, the sight, the taste of her all melt into one coherent object representation in his memory.

And now I wish to advance this proposition: Achieving such a coherent and structured object representation is the indispensable prerequisite for establishing object constancy. Once stated this seems self-evident. And so it is—but only for sighted children. Once they can nurse with open eyes they stare continuously at the mother's face while at her breast. It is, then, the sight of this face which provides continuity. It permits the child to become gradually aware that the nipple still exists, even when his lips do not touch it, even when the milk is not flowing into his mouth. Vision provides the lasting link with the need-gratifying situation (breast nursing) by adding distance perception to contact perception. By the third month the child's visual discrimination has matured sufficiently and the visual percepts are sufficiently associated with the relief of being nursed, diapered, and so on, so that the infant remembers a total Gestalt. Every element of this Gestalt, such as the sound of mother's voice or the sight of her will evoke pleasant memories of need gratification. The infant smiles on beholding the mere face because it signals milk. Thus for the sighted child the need-gratifying object never disappear. For in the absence of real gratification there is always hope that good things will happen again, and that makes waiting tolerable. Thus frustration tolerance starts.

From here on and in an ever-increasing measure, vision becomes the leading perceptual modality for reality testing, for adaptation, for the organizing of the surround, and for the registering of all this in the child's memory banks.

At this juncture we must take a detour: How does a blind-born child develop? Here we must pay attention to a seemingly minor developmental step recently discovered by Selma Fraiberg. It is the child's ability to reach, guided by vision, for animate or inanimate objects. He will manipulate them and in a way get acquainted with them by touch and grasp. Fraiberg demonstrated observationally how in sighted children grasping leads ultimately to locomotion. The blind-born child, however, lacks the incentive for reaching and therefore does not spontaneously learn to walk.

My proposition regarding the establishment of the libidinal object (mother) around the eighth month of life anticipated in a rather hazy manner the findings I have just described. At that time I had suggested that during the first six months the so-called good and bad mother appeared to the child as if they were two separate objects. The one cathected primarily by the libidinal, the other by the aggressive drive. I further suggested that in the course of the mother's reciprocal affective relations with her child, the visual percept of her face provided that unbroken continuity which finally achieves the fusion of the two maternal images and the two drives, and the mother appears as one and the same person (The libidinal object, Spitz 1953). This fusion comes about in the second half of the first year of life, on the average after the sixth and before the end of the eighth month.

How do we know that fusion of the two mother images has indeed occurred and that the baby has reached a higher level of integration? The indicator is the eighth-month anxiety (Spitz 1950). A word about this phenomenon. Children of approximately eight months very clearly distinguish between the mother's face and the faces of comparative strangers. The latter ones are being viewed with an apprehensive frown or a tearful outburst, whereas the mother's face evokes a smile or at least an expression of complacency. The role of vision in this developmental step is manifest. Incidentally and by way of a proof for the above theory, the discomfort an infant shows when approached by a stranger can be relieved as soon as the stranger turns his back on the infant. When he is not forced to see the frightening face, the baby can relax.

At this point we may well ask: What is it that distinguishes vision from the other sensory modalities? There are four factors:

1) *The quantitative factor:* Vision transmits the objects of our environment continuously, conveying many more consciously perceived bits of information than all other senses together. The data, at least for the infant, remain the same for long stretches of time (the same window, blanket, highchair in the same spots); they are perceived simultaneously, yet they are individually distinct coherent entities. The observing child finds himself among the data, that is, he observes parts of himself as if they were outside objects.

2) *The qualitative factor:* As the objects change in space, it is vision and only vision that can endow a particular thing with meaning and continuity. (Yesterday the highchair was was right next to the window, today it is in the opposite corner of the room. One can sit on it and it has a red padding . . . no matter in which corner it stands.) Vision and only vision reconciles the permanence of objects with their impermanence in space. And finally only vision can transform the objects which are perceived into a coherent continuous and gap-free universe. Touch, taste, smell, even hearing transmit only fragments of our world. Vision alone has integrating and organizing properties.

3) *The Gestalt quality:* Vision has certain Gestalt attributes. To see means to distinguish between figure and background and to have a tendency toward the completion gradient, toward closure, toward transposing elements of one Gestalt

to other places. Above all, to see means to perceive movement. Nothing defines a Gestalt as well as its movement against a stationary background—and vice versa. To perceive movement enables us to anticipate gratification. It also alerts us to danger. To see movement therefore serves survival.

4) *The cause-effect quality:* Vision, as we stated before, affords the child an unbroken succession of percepts. This in turn enforces the experience of a rational universe in which "B" regularly follows "A." That makes vision the only one of our senses to convey the logical sequence of cause and effect. Vision therefore helps overcome magical thinking and fosters the reality principle.

In this connection vision also plays an essential role in the mother-child relationship, as during the first sixteen weeks it links the person to the relief which she brings. Toward the end of the first year it is, of course, vision that makes it possible for the child to model himself after the mother and to ultimately identify with her. Thus vision is a precondition for the internalized conscience.

The affective interchange between mother and child, which we call here Fundamental Education, leads to many more developmental achievements, some of which appear to grown-ups as easy as breathing. They must, however, be acquired by the infant and later on in childhood, sometimes the hard way. Among these achievements is a sense of identity and a sense of responsibility for himself, by which, in the words of Anna Freud (1936), "he takes over from his mother, caring for himself." Years later this sense of responsibility will help in the formation of the superego and make him a full-fledged grade schooler and later high school student. It should, however, be stated that by the time a child has acquired the primordia of morality the essence of Fundamental Education has changed. The mother's original permissiveness, so appropriate during the first year of life, has been replaced by many dos and don'ts. The mother's more or less strict demands go against the child's newly acquired autonomy and his newly established self. His refusals to comply result in further maternal prohibitions and disciplinary efforts. These conflicts between mother and child are, however, necessary components of Fundamental Education for the sake of the next developmental steps.

One such step is toilet training. Another step, though often overlooked by us, is the fact that even during the toddler stage a child must be able to focus his attention, however briefly, on others; that he must have learned without too much anxiety or hostility a certain minimum of social adjustment to his peers as well as to adults. The fact one almost never thinks of is that the child must have *learned to learn* the above skills; that through the ongoing dialogue with his mother he must have become *desirous* and *capable* of learning; that once Fundamental Education has awakened his curiosity, it must stay alive; that his eagerness for identification must make it possible for him to become like his peers. Fundamental Education and the resulting urge to identify with others will make the child went to talk; to experiment with the magic of words; to understand the spell which the all-powerful teacher exercises when she makes the unruly class comply; to master the seemingly meaningless signs which the teacher has drawn on the blackboard. For these signs begin to live as the teacher draws a *C*, an *A*, and a *T* on the board, and it turns into *cat;* and a *B*, an *O*, and a *B* and, lo and behold, the word stands for the little boy who is deciphering it. If Fundamental Education has been powerful enough to achieve all these feats, then the little boy, all things being equal, will not become a dropout. Instead he will assimilate what school teaches him and will use it in various ways, first for developing an ego, then a self.

Fundamental Education is a necessary condition for all learning, but it is precarious and exposed to many possible dangers, some of which I have mentioned earlier: hospitalism, anaclitic depression, blindness from birth, failure to grasp, and others. Also it is endangered by a pervasive syndrome which has been called the disadvantaged child syndrome. Disadvantaged children, when placed into Headstart centers often make progress, appear to overcome their language handicap, and perform well in regard to the whole curriculum in an age-appropriate manner.

But, upon entering grade school, they often seem to lose the gain they have made and regress to the level to those poverty children who had never attended Headstart. We may well ask ourselves what the reasons for this failure might be. I am inclined to assume that children growing up in stark poverty are often deprived of Fundemental Education from the beginning, and develop the "learning *not* to learn" syndrome. This hypothesis, however, offers only a partial explanation. Another factor seems to be that of critical periods. The concept of critical periods was developed by Scott (1950) as the result of experiments on dogs. I had developed at the same time a similar concept on the basis of infant observation. The hypothesis of critical periods postulates that development of certain functions takes place at specific optimal age periods of limited duration. Their chronology and sequence seems to be innate. In other words critical periods are time stretches during which the organism is ready to respond to specific stimuli. If these stimuli are not forthcoming when they should be, then the responses either won't occur at all, or else they will require a far greater effort and a longer time to develop than would ordinarily be the case.

The hypothesis of critical periods has been checked in the last twenty years in a large number of experiments and finds an ever-widening application in developmental psychology. In animal psychology it applies to the phenomenon of imprinting; also, as in the following example, to the development of perceptual modalities. Huber and Wiesel performed an experiment in which they sealed the eyelids of kittens at birth and kept them sealed for a period of eighteen months. Thereafter the kittens' eyes were unsealed, but to no avail, for they never learned to see. A second set of kittens was subjected to the same experiment, however at a different time schedule. This second set of animals were permitted to use their eyes for the first three months of their lives and thereafter had their lids sealed for the identical period as the first group, namely for fourteen to eighteen months. Once their eyes were unsealed the second group promptly regained their sight.

In human beings the phenomenon of critical periods seems to be either less spectacular or perhaps has not been sufficiently observed. There are, however, some developmental achievements which clearly depend on critical periods. Among them are the abilities to grasp and to reach (Fraiberg), which ultimately lead to locomotion and to the acquisition of verbal facilities. Also, the concept of critical periods applies, as I was able to show, to the phenomenon of hospitalism. Severe emotional deprivation between six and fifteen months will lead to basic deficiencies in human beings which are irreparable.

Accordingly my proposition is this: The child who is deprived of Fundamental Education during the first year of life will, depending on the specific age level and the duration of the deprivation, suffer from inadequate or arrested development of certain age-specific functions.

For our present purposes and in connection with Headstart and similar enterprises, the most important problems seem to be these: Which sector of the first year is the critical period for the acquisition of speech? Which for thought processes? Which for "learning to learn"? If the critical periods exist, if they are as specific as I have assumed, then insufficient Fundamental Education will lead to lasting impairment in areas vital for learning in general. The so-called normal children in the population include large numbers of children who are thus impaired for economic or social reasons. For these children we will have to find methods to insure that they also receive their birthright. Such an enterprise requires a vast amount of research. At present we know only vaguely what elements go into Fundamental Education. We do, however, know that any circumstance, infirmity, or other condition limiting communication between mother and child is a damaging factor, interrupting a developmental line. The resulting deficit does not yield to ordinary teaching methods but will require special remedial techniques as yet undiscovered. What is equally needed is a description of the minute details of affective reciprocity between mother and child, so that impairment in critical periods can be prevented, so that every child can receive Fundamental Education. For Fundamental Education is needed to transform the little bundle of helpless, mindless living matter into a human being; into a social being; into a fellow being—into our brother.

BIBLIOGRAPHY

Baldwin, J. M. *Dictionary of Philosophy and Psychology*. New York: Peter Smith, 1940.

Emde, R. N., and Metcalf, D. "An EEG Study of Behavioral Rapid Eye Movement States in the Human Newborn." *J. Nervous and Mental Diseases* 150 (1969): 376–86.

Fraiberg, S., and Freedman, D. A. "Studies in the Ego Development of the Congenitally Blind Child." *Psychoanalytic Study of the Child* 19 (1964): 113–69.

Goodlad, J. T. "How Do We Learn." *Saturday Review*, June 21, 1969, pp. 74–75, 85–86.

Polak, P. Personal communication.

Polak, P.; Emde, R. N.; and Spitz, R. A. "Smiling Response of the Human Face. I. Methodology. Quantification and Natural History." *J. Nervous & Mental Dis.* 139, no. 2 (1964).

Provence, S., and Lipton, R. C. *Infants in Institutions: A Comparison of Their Development with Family-Reared Infants during the First Year of Life*. New York: International Universities Press, 1962.

Scott, J. P., and Marston, M. W. "Critical Periods of Affecting the Development of Normal and Maladaptive Social Behavior of Puppies." *J. Genet. Psychol.* 77 (1950): 25–59.

Spencer, H. *Essays on Education*, 1861.

Spitz, R. A. "Aggression: Its Roles in the Establishment of Object Relations." In *Drives, Affects, Behavior*, edited by R. M. Loewenstein, pp. 126–38. New York: International Universities Press, 1953.

Spitz, R. A. "Anxiety in Infancy: A Study of Its Manifestations in the First Year of Life." *Int. J. of Psychoanalysis* 31 (1950): 138–43.

Spitz, R. A. *The First Year of Life: Normal and Deviant Object Relations*. New York: International Universities Press, 1965.

Spitz, R. A. "Primal Cavity: A Contribution to the Genesis of Perception and Its Role for Psychoanalytic Theory." *Psychoanalytic Study of the Child* 10 (1955): 215–40.

Spitz, R. A., and Wolf, K. M. "The Smiling Response," *Genetic Psychology Monographs* 34 (1946): 57–125.

KONRAD LORENZ

The Enmity between Generations and Its Probable Ethological Causes

I. DARWINIAN APPROACH AND THE QUESTION OF ADAPTATION

"Ethology" is simply the application to the field of behavior study of all those methods of approach which, since the days of Charles Darwin, are regarded as obligatory in all other branches of biological research. In other words, ethology regards behavior as a *system* which owes its existence and its special form to a series of historical events which have taken place in the course of phylogeny. The purely causal question *why* a living system happens to be structured as it is and not otherwise cannot be answered except by investigating the history of its evolution, in other words its *phylogeny*.

Investigating behavior, including human behavior, from the

phylogenetical viewpoint has brought ethology into the center of an ideological controversy which is still going on. The doctrine that human behavior is entirely determined by processes of conditioning which are brought about by environmental influence, originated from an immoderate generalization and simplification of the findings of I. P. Pavlov. It became the basic theory of American behaviorism, yet it would imply injustice and even slander to call it the "behavioristic" doctrine, because many intelligent scientists who consider themselves "behaviorists" have never believed in it. I therefore suggest the term "pseudodemocratic" doctrine. This is justified by the fact that the doctrine derives its worldwide distribution as well as its moral weight from the rather insidious distortion of a democratic truth: it is a truth and indubitably a moral postulate that all men should have equal opportunities to develop. But an untrue dogma is easily derived from that truth (if only by those that reject logic, as Philip Wylie has pointed out): that all men are potentially equal. The doctrine carries the premise one step further by asserting that man is born as a *tabula rasa* and that all his behavior is determined by conditioning.

Ethology has run foul of this doctrine by demonstrating irrefutably that all behavior, exactly like all bodily structure, can develop in the ontogeny of the individual only along the lines and within the possibilities of species-specific programs which have been mapped out in the course of phylogeny and laid down in the code of the genome. "Biology," says Philip Wylie, "has proven that men are not equal, identical, similar or anything of the sort, from the instant of conception. Common sense ought to have made all that evident to Java man. It didn't and still doesn't, since common sense is what men most passionately wish to evade." This passion has the character of truly religious zeal. The pseudodemocratic doctrine has indeed become a world religion. Like many religions, it is the simplification of a truth, as such easy to understand, and it is welcome to those that are interested in manipulating great masses of people. It would indeed be of equal advantage to capitalistic producers and to super-Stalinistic rulers, if men, by proper conditioning, could be molded into absolutely uniform and absolutely obedient consumers or communistic citizens. This explains the otherwise surprising fact that the pseudodemocratic doctrine rules supreme in America as well as in the Soviet Union and in China!

Like all devout supports of a religion, the doctrinaires of the pseudodemocratic doctrine do not stop at anything when it comes to silencing the heretic. The approach to human behavior as to a phylogenetically evolved system has been rejected on a large number of pseudorational reasons and branded as immoral in a large number of ways, of which the book *Man and Aggression*, edited by M. F. Ashley Montagu offers a rich choice of examples, of which one is sufficient to demonstrate the near-religious bias. "There is," says Ashley Montagu, "not the slightest evidence or ground for assuming that the alleged 'phylogenetically adapted instinctive' behaviour of other animals is in any way relevant to the discussion of the motive-forces of human behaviour. The fact is, that with the exception of the instinctoid reactions of infants to sudden withdrawals of support and to sudden loud noises, the human being is entirely instinctless." More modern representatives of the pseudodemocratic doctrine take another and more subtle attitude. While conceding that ethology is, in principle, correct in trying to separate phylogenetically evolved and ontogenetically acquired programs of behavior, they contend that ethologists attribute an exaggerated importance to this distinction, in other words, that the question "innate or acquired?" is no more than a quibble. It isn't and I shall come back to this point at the end of this paper.

For the moment it suffices to say that most of the properties which we encounter in the structure as well as in the behavior of organisms owe their specific form to that oldest and most efficient of cognitive processes, which we call *adaptation*. The fact of adaptedness entails a question characteristic of biology and unknown to chemistry and physics, the question "what for?". When we ask, "What for has the cat crooked retractile claws?" and answer, "To catch mice with," we are not questing for the ultimate teleological meaning of the cat's claws, we are only using an abridged way of expressing a truly scientific *causal* question which, fully stated, should read: "What is the function whose survival value exerted the selection pressure *causing* cats to evolve that particular form of claws?".

A lifetime spent in asking this question (to which I shall refer to henceforward as Charles Darwin's question) with reference to a great many morphological structures and behavior patterns results in great support for Darwin's theories, for the simple reason that so very, very often a clear-cut and convincing answer can be found. In fact, we have grown so accustomed to receiving such an answer that we find it hard to believe that there *are* any highly complex and differentiated patterns or structures which do *not* owe their specific form to the selection pressure exerted by their function. The more bizarre they appear on their face value, the surer one may be of discovering such a function.

II. CREATIVE INTEGRATION AND THE METHOD OF APPROACHING SYSTEMS

Before expounding the methods obligatory in the approach of complex systems, a few words must be said about the way in which unprecedented systematic properties spring into existence when two pre-existent but independent systems are linked together; if, for instance, two systems of electric circuit, one running over a coil, the other obstructed by a condenser, are linked together, the new system will possess the property of oscillation, which is not to be found, on principle, in any of the two subsystems in their unconnected state. This kind of event obviously has happened and is happening whenever phylogenesis makes a step forward. The term *evolution*, as well as the German word *Entwicklung*, implies etymologically that something *performed* is merely being unfolded in the process. None of our Western languages possesses a verb for the coming-into-existence of something entirely new, because at the time of their origin, the only process of development known was that of ontogeny, for which these terms are indeed etymologically adequate. Sensing its inadequacy for the creative events of phylogeny, some philosophers used the term *emergence*, which is still worse, as it implies that something which was invisible only to a literally superficial view becomes visible by surfacing. In my paper "Innate Bases of Learning," in which I discussed these matters in detail, I suggested to use, in a new sense, the term *fulguration*, which had been introduced by medieval mystics to describe acts of creation, implying, of course, that it was God's own lightning that caused something new to spring into existence. For the scientist, lightning is an electric spark like any other, and if he notices an unexpected spark within a system, the first thing it brings to mind is a short circuit. This makes the term *fulguration* strangely appropriate. That which constitutes a step forward in the sequence of creative phylogenetic events regularly consists in the coming-into-existence of a new systemic property which is caused by a new causal relationship springing up, within the living system, between two of its pre-existing subsystems, integrating them into a new one of higher order. As we refuse to believe in miracles, we are convinced that it is always a structural change that brings about such a new integration and causes laws of nature which had not previously existed to come into existence.

The new lawfulness arising out of new structures never abolishes the laws of nature prevailing within the living system previous to the new event of integration. Even the systemic properties of the newly united subsystems need not be entirely lost. This is true of every step taken by evolution, even of its greatest and initial step from the inorganic to the organic. It is quite particularly true of what we, in admitted pride, are apt to consider the second greatest step, the one leading from the anthropoid to Man. The processes of life are still physical and chemical processes, though by virtue of the complicated structure of chain molecules, they are something very particular besides. It would be plain nonsense to assert that they are "nothing else but" chemical and physical processes. An analogous relationship exists between man and his prehuman ancestors: man certainly is an animal but it is simply not true that he is nothing but an animal.

III. CUMULATIVE TRADITION AS AN EXAMPLE

The fulguration of those properties which are essential of man and which do not exist, at least not together and not to any appreciable degree, in any other animal furnishes an excellent example of the way in which new systematic properties come into existence with new connections of pre-existing systems. Exploratory behavior leading to a considerable degree of objective knowledge of objects exists in many animals and so does true tradition of individually acquired knowledge. In Man alone they are brought together into an integrated system.

Self-exploration, which had been dawning in the anthropoids, must have progressed by leaps and bounds as our forefathers proceded from tool-using to tool-making. The working hand, as a part of the own body, together with the manipulated object in the same visual field could not fail to draw attention to the fact that one's own subject is also an object, and one extremely worthy of consideration! By the consciousness of his own self, by "reflection," a new objectivity was forced upon man's attitude to the objects of his environment. Originally, and for the majority of all animals, one object possesses entirely different meanings dependent on the different psychological and physiological states in which the organism happens to be at the moment. A potential prey animal has entirely different "valences" for a hungry lion and for a satiated one. Once we have realized that we are ourselves "real things" participating in an interaction with the other "things" in our environment, we have automatically gained a higher and altogether new level of objectivity transcending by far that which had hitherto been possible by virtue of the abstracting function of Gestalt perception and by the effects of exploratory play. Not being hungry, we might be totally uninterested in a food object and pass it by as the sated lion does, but knowing ourselves as we do, we are able to take our own momentary state into consideration and abstract from it, rightly foreseeing that the object in question may and will become highly interesting in a short while.

It is only together with and on the basis of all the other objective functions which already pre-existed in higher animals that true reflection could come into being. Self-exploration could never have happened except on the basis of a pre-existing, highly developed exploratory behavior. The comprehension of a concept could never have been achieved had it not been for the observation of the own prehensile hand taking hold of and interacting with environmental objects.

Tradition existed before that. Rats can pass on the knowledge concerning the deadly effects of a poison over many generations without any individual repeating the personal experience leading to that knowledge. Jackdaws can hand down to the unexperienced young their knowledge of dangerous predators, and monkeys have been known to pass on the tradition of certain acquired motor skills, for instance that of washing sweet potatoes in sea water. However, all these processes of the handing-down of acquired knowledge are dependent on the presence of their object. Without it, the rat cannot tell its young what poison not to eat, nor can the jackdaw teach its progeny what predator to avoid, nor the monkey demonstrate its skill. Even so, we cannot quite explain why traditional knowledge does not tend to accumulate in any species of social animal beyond the degree to which we actually find it developed. Thus, right up to the fulguration of cumulative tradition in man, the genome remained the only mechanism capable of an accumulating long-time storage of knowledge.

With the coming-together of conceptual thought and tradition, unprecedented systemic properties sprang into existence. The continuity of tradition made it possible for concepts to become associated with the free symbol of the spoken word. The growth of syntactic language was thus rendered possible, and, in turn, opened a new avenue to an accumulation of traditional knowledge, ever increasing with the number of generations following one another. The new system is that which is generally called culture and its unique systemic property consists in its being able, like the genome, to store practically unlimited quantities of information and, at the same time, being able, unlike the genome, to acquire knowledge worth storing within minutes instead of millennia. If a man learns how to make or invents a bow and arrow, not only his progeny but all his culture will henceforward possess these tools, nor is the likelihood of their ever being forgotten any greater than that of a bodily organ of equal survival value ever becoming rudimentary. The new systemic property is neither more nor less than the famous inheritance of acquired characters and its biological consequences are hard to exaggerate. It was the selection pressure of accumulating tradition which caused man's telencephalon to grow to its present size. It is bodily structures, such as the forebrain and the various speech areas in the dominant hemisphere which make man *by nature* a creature of culture. Without cultural tradition, these structures would be as devoid of function as the wings of an ostrich, only more so. Yet all these tremendous changes, which certainly do make man something that is very different indeed from that which we would describe as "just an animal," were wrought by the rather simple integration of two subsystems of behavior, none of which is exclusively characteristic of our species.

Our knowledge of the way in which, during phylogeny, systems of higher integration came into being by a series of unique and unpredictable historic events, has far-reaching consequences in two entirely unrelated respects.

IV. THE AXIOMATIC SCALE OF ORGANISMIC VALUES

The first concerns our philosophy of values. We cannot help feeling that organic systems are the more valuable the more highly integrated they are, in fact our accustomed way of calling some animals higher and some lower is the immediate outcome of this inescapable value judgment. Its axiomatic nature is easily demonstrated by the following thought-experiment. Visualize yourself confronted with the task of killing, one after the other, a cabbage, a fly, a fish, a lizard, a guinea pig, a cat, a dog, a monkey, and a baby chimpanzee. In the unlikely case that you should experience no greater inhibitions in killing the chimpanzee than in destroying the cabbage or the fly, my advice to you is to commit suicide at your earliest possible convenience, because you are a weird monstrosity and a public danger.

The scale of values extending between lower and higher organisms is quite independent of that other which stretches between all the degrees of less and more successful adaptation to environment. The chances of disadaptation and illness are roughly the same on all levels of creative integration; if anything, the higher creatures seem to be more vulnerable than the lower. A man or, for that matter, a whole culture may be in direct danger of disintegration and yet be of higher value than another which is in the best possible state of health and superlatively viable. We are apt to become aware of the independence of the two parameters of value judgment when we come to consider our own moral responsibility. Obedience to the moral law within us, as Immanuel Kant has called it, may often exact a behavior which is far from healthy and not too rarely human beings are faced with the alternative of either

behaving immorally or making the great sacrifice of martyr-
dom—which may in addition be entirely in vain.

V. METHODS OBLIGATORY IN THE APPROACH TO INTEGRATED SYSTEMS

The second all-important consequence which is forced upon
us by the realization of the "stratified" structure of organic
systems concerns the strategy of their analysis. For obvious
reasons, the first step to the understanding of a system which
consists of a whole hierarchy of subsystems, integrated into
each other level by level, must be to gain some provisional sur-
vey knowledge of those subsystems which, on the highest
level of integration, are immediately subordinate to the whole.
To begin with this first task is the more obligatory, the more
complicated and the more highly integrated the system under
investigation actually is. In other words, the chances of gaining insight into the make-up of a system by atomistic and op-
erationalist methods decreases in proportion to its complication
and its level of integration. We must be successful in quite a
few inspired guesses in order to arrive even at that prehypo-
thetical stage of vague suspicion which allows us to sift our
observations sufficiently to arrive at a workable hypothesis as
to what are the greatest and most widely embracing subsystems to approach. In this task, plain observation and the free
play of our own Gestalt perception are the most promising
methods. I wish to assert seriously and emphatically that in
our first tentative approach to the understanding of complicated living systems, the "visionary" approach of the poet—
which consists simply in letting Gestalt perception rule supreme—gets us much farther than any pseudoscientific mea-
suring of arbitrarily chosen parameters. I do not mean that a

man who is "nothing else but" a poet has a better chance of understanding integrated systems than a scientist has. What I want to express is that a scientist, with all the scientist's methodological and factual knowledge at his disposal, has no chance of ever understanding a complex living system such as that underlying human social behavior unless he utilizes his Gestalt perception to the utmost, giving it an absolutely free rein while at the same time feeding into its ample hold as many pertinent observational data as he can get hold of. There are people who seem to be able to do just that. One of them is Erik Erikson, who, in my opinion, knows more about the deepest roots of human behavior than anybody else I could name.

VI. PATHOLOGICAL DISTURBANCE AS A SOURCE OF KNOWLEDGE

Even so, Gestalt perception would not lead us far enough in the understanding of really complex systems like that of human behavior to make it possible to begin applying the quantitative methods of verification, were it not for help from a rather unexpected side.

There are cases in which Charles Darwin's question "What for?" fails to get an answer. In captive animals and quite particularly in civilized men we find regularly recurring behavior patterns which are not only devoid of value but even demonstrably detrimental to the survival of the individual as well as of the species. If one asks Darwin's question with regard to a military parade, a voodoo ceremony in Haiti, a sit-in of students at a Vienna university, or modern war, one finds oneself unable to obtain an answer—at least as long as one applies the question in the simple and unsophisticated way in which, as biologists, we are accustomed to put it.

When confronted with such a puzzling and disturbing behavior pattern, my late friend Bernhard Hellmann used to ask another question: "Is this as the constructor intended it to be?" Though this question was asked half-jestingly, it implies a deep realization of the existence of a border line which, though extremely difficult to define, plays an all-important role in biological and particularly in medical thought: the border line between the normal and the pathological, between health and illness.

When, in respect to some crazy pattern of human behavior, we fail to get an answer to Charles Darwin's question "What for?" as well as to Bernhard Hellmann's question "Is this how the constructor meant it to be?" we need not lose confidence in normal biological approach, though we have to resort to additional questions belonging to a different way of approach, to that of the medical man. In one of his last letters to me, my late friend Ronald Hargreaves, psychiatrist at Leeds, wrote that he had schooled himself to ask, in approaching any sort of mental disorder, two simultaneous questions. The first is: What is the normal survival function of the process here disturbed? The second is: What is the nature of the disturbance, and, in particular, is there an excess or a deficiency of the function in question?

At first sight it might seem that the unpredictable pathological disturbance of a system which is superlatively complicated and, therefore, most difficult to understand in any case would add yet another and unsurmountable obstruction to the endeavor of its analysis. However, physiologists have known for a long time that this is not so. So far from being an additional obstacle to the analysis of a system, its pathological disturbance is, as often as not, the key to its analysis. In fact, the history of physiology has recorded a great number of cases in which the very existence of an important physiological mechanism or system was not even suspected until an illness caused by the disturbance of one of them drew the scientists' attention to it. The history of the discovery of endocrine glands and of the progress of their analysis offers an excellent paradigm of the method obligatory in approaching systems. When E. T. Kocher, in the attempt of curing hyperthyroidism, had removed the thyroid gland, he found that he had provoked what he termed *cachexia thyropriva*. From this he deduced correctly that the function of the thyroid gland stood in a relation of balanced antagonism with that of other endocrine glands and that Basedow's disease, or hyperthyroidism, consisted in the disturbance of this equilibrium in favor of an excess of thyroid function.

The rationale of this approach is most strictly applicable to the majority of the disturbances nowadays observable in the social behavior of human beings. Indeed very many of them consist in the loss of equilibrium between two or more behavioral systems, the word *system* being used in the sense of the excellent definition Paul Weiss has given in his paper "Determinism Stratified": a system is everything unitary enough to deserve a name. Ronald Hargreaves's double question ought to make everybody realize how inane it is to attribute the adjectives *good* or *bad* to any mechanism of behavior, such as love, aggression, indoctrination, ritualization, enthusiasm, and so on. Like any endocrine gland, every one of these mechanisms is indispensable and, again like a gland, every one, by its excess function, can lead to a destructive disequilibration. There is no human vice which is anything else than the excess of a function which, in itself, is indispensable for the survival of the species.

I shall now proceed to illustrate the application of Ronald Hargreaves's double question to certain phenomena which are obviously threatening our culture and which, in my opinion, can be attributed to the disequilibration, of two important behavioral systems. The first is the mechanism which ensures that which Sigmund Freud described as the balanced economy of pleasure and displeasure. The second is the rather complicated system whose function it is to transmit traditional knowledge from one generation to the next while at the same time making sure that obsolete items of tradition can be discarded and new ones acquired.

VII. THE DISEQUILIBRATON OF PLEASURE-DISPLEASURE ECONOMY

I begin with the description of some symptoms which I believe to be caused by the disturbance of pleasure-displeasure equilibrium. Perhaps the most telling of these symptoms is the *urge for instant gratification*. In a considerable percentage of present-day humanity, and not only among the younger generation, there is a demonstrable decrease in the ability and willingness to strive for aims that can only be achieved in the future. Any goal that cannot be attained *at once* ceases to appear worth striving for. Even large business concerns refuse to look more than a very few years into the future. In science the unwillingness to undertake long-term programs has led to a deplorable neglect of *descriptive* branches in which a patient and protracted gathering of knowledge is necessary.

Although it is not clear which is cause and which is effect, there is certainly a close connection between the current loss of patience and a general *inability to endure any kind of pain or displeasure*. The enormous consumption of anodynes and tranquilizers bears witness to this intolerance. Once I observed my nephew swallowing an enormous spoonful of pyramidon powder and commiseratingly asked him whether he had got a bad headache. No, he said, but he was somewhat afraid that he might get one. Kurt Hahn tells a story about a pupil coming to school carrying with him a package of tablets which his parents had given him and which were guaranteed to be an unfailing cure against any onset of homesickness.

A third queer symptom, closely allied to the two already mentioned, is a general *unwillingness to move*. Any exertion of striated musculature has become unfashionable, to the point of changing the facial expression of large numbers of people: a tired, languishing, bored look, occasionally slightly overlaid by an expression of reproach and sulkiness is observable in all too many young people. Between the twenty-year-olds of, say 1920 and those of 1969, there is a very considerable behavioral difference in the quantity of locomotion performed for its own sake. In the Vienna Woods, which were teeming with young people in 1920, one rarely meets walkers, and if one does, they are over sixty. Amongst young people who consider themselves as very sporting, there may be a certain willingness to perform muscular labor, but only for its own sake and not in pursuance of any other goal. This would be considered as "work." Therefore, athletic young people can be seen queuing-up for forty minutes at a ski lift in favor of walking uphill for twenty.

Technological production caters to the growing unwillingness to perform muscular work; a prosperous citizen cannot be expected to walk upstairs or to turn a crank to open a window or the sliding roof of his smart car: to press a button is the utmost he will condescend to do.

It was Kurt Hahn who called attention to the disquieting fact that this type of physical laziness is very often correlated with an accompanying *sluggishness of emotion*. A weakness of ability to feel *compassion* is, according to the great expert, a frequent concomitant of the typical laziness of blasé adolescents. I do not think I need mention examples, every daily paper is full of instances in which people have been tortured, killed, or raped in well-frequented streets of big cities in the presence of hosts of inhumans who refused to "get involved" by assisting the victim. Inability to feel compassion also plays an important part in the acts of open hostility against weak old people of which adolescents often are guilty.

Now let us ask, in respect to the phenomena just described, the first of the two questions proposed by Ronald Hargreaves. What is the normal function which is miscarrying in each of these cases and what is the nature of its miscarriage? I think we can give a fairly probable tentative answer to these questions, and what is more, the same applies to all four of the phenomena mentioned.

All organisms capable of true conditioning possess a built-in mechanism whose function it is to mete out reward and punishment, reward for behavior achieving survival value for the individual or the species, or both, and punishment for all that is contrary to these interests. *Reward* and *punishment* are terms here used only as shorthand for the functions of *reinforcing or extinguishing* the preceding behavior. Pleasure and displeasure are the equally real subjective experiences which accompany these learning processes.

Many otherwise profound theories on learning have overlooked a fact which is of supreme importance to our consideration, namely that this highly integrated computing mechanism must possess in its program phylogenetically acquired information, in fact *knowledge of what is good and what is bad for the organism*. This mechanism "knows" all the values of reference which all the homoeostatic cycles within the organism are supposed to keep constant; it administers the punishment of making us feel lousy if anything is out of order in any of these regulating cycles, for instance if we have too little or too much oxygen, glucose, or whatever else in our blood, if we are too hot or too cold, and so on. It rewards us by making us feel good whenever our behavior has contributed to correct these values, as we do when we ingest the right kind of food, and so on. It puts a premium on performing any of the typical species-preserving activities in the biologically "right" manner.

This great teaching mechanism, the "innate schoolmarm," as I have jestingly called it, could, theoretically, work with reward (or reinforcement) alone, or with punishment (or extinguishing) alone. We have introspective knowledge, however, that it uses *both* principles and there are objective criteria supporting the assumption that the same is true of animals. It would be that it is just a case of assurance being made doubly sure, a procedure of which there are many examples in evolution. Another tentative answer, which I thought sufficient until quite recently, lies in the fact that it is difficult to make organisms behave in a very *specific* manner by the exclusive use of repellent stimuli. It is very hard to *drive* a bird into a cage, as one would have to use a large number of stimuli impinging from all spatial directions with the exception of that of the cage door to do so. Thus it would seem preferable to put some reward into the cage and thus entice the creature to enter it. We find that evolution has learned that trick and "applies" extinguishing procedures if the biological aim is just to keep an animal away from noxious environmental influences, but "uses" the allurement of reinforcement in cases in which the organism is requested to do something more specific.

A further difference between reinforcing and extinguishing processes lies in the manner in which external stimulation is evaluated. In appetitive behavior, in which the organism is endeavoring to reach the source of stimulation, any increase in the quantity of incoming stimuli acts as a reinforcement, while in avoidance behavior any decrease in stimulation reinforces the preceding mode of behavior.

These considerations are quite correct, as far as they go, yet they do not contain the real answer to the question why the conditioning apparatus of higher animals is constructed on the basis of two opposing principles. The antagonistic effect of two independently variable motivations is necessary to uphold an *economic* equilibrium between certain biological advantages gained and the expenses incurred in gaining them. By virtue of conditioning, the organism is made capable of going straight for the achievement of some goal which has survival value and which offers a *future* reward, in spite of the fact that it has to begin its activity in the teeth of a *present* stimulus situation acting as a strongly extinguishing deterrent.

It is this element of *foresight* that constitutes the most important function of conditioning. It enables the organism to pay a price for something to be gained later, the price consisting of the expenditure of energy, of incurring certain risks and other disadvantages. The balance of pleasure and displeasure, all the phenomena which Sigmund Freud called *Lust-Ökonomie* represent the subjective side of that kind of deal.

If this negotiation is to yield, to the organism or its species, a net gain in terms of survival value, the price paid must be in proportion to the gain in gross value it purchases. It would be bad strategy for a wolf to go hunting, regardless of the cold, in a particularly bad winter's night; he simply could not afford to pay for one meal with a frozen toe or two. However, circumstances may arise, for instance a dire famine, in which our wolf would indeed be well advised to go hunting regardless of costs and risks, playing a single, last chance.

This example serves to illustrate that there is no constant relationship between the values of the goal achieved and the price paid for its achievement. Exactly as in commercial economy, the price which is to be considered as adequate in a given situation is determined by the laws of supply and demand. The varying strength of the motivations causing appetitive behavior is to a great extent determined by the *needs* of the organism or the species—very often indeed in a most direct manner by the tissue needs of the individual. The effectiveness which the achievement of the goal develops *as a reinforcement* of the preceding behavior varies in proportion to the strength of this motivation. The readiness to tolerate punishment which is unavoidable in the conquering of obstacles does exactly the same. It is an immensely complicated and finely adjusted system of adaptively variable reinforcing and extinguishing mechanisms which achieve a balanced equilibrium in the organism's economy.

I believe that we can unhesitatingly answer Ronald Hargreaves's first question concerning the survival function of the disturbed mechanism by saying that the symptoms hitherto discussed—the inability to wait, the inability to bear displeasure, the unwillingness to move, and the weakness of compassionate emotion—all are caused by a disturbance of the mechanism achieving the balanced equilibrium of pleasure-displeasure economy.

I proceed to Hargreaves's second question: What is the nature of the disturbance? In order to make my tentative answer intelligible, I must say a few more words about the physiological as well as the historical properties of this balancing mechanism.

Like many other neurosensory functions, the mechanism under discussion is subject to habituation or "sensory adaptation." This term, though generally accepted by sense physiologists, is not a happy choice, because the effect of the phenomenon need not necessarily be adaptive in the sense of survival. The *waning* of the response to an often-repeated stimulus—or combination of stimuli—is advantageous only on the premise of the statistical probability that an ever-recurrent stimulus is not likely to denote something really important. Whatever it signals is likely to be rather "cheap" economically. In some respects, habituation may be similar to fatigue and it may even have evolved phylogenetically from certain forms of fatigue. Its function, however, is entirely different. Also, habituation is not localized in the peripheral sense organ, but, as Margret Schleidt has shown experimentally, in the central nervous system itself. Habituation is not always specific to one particular stimulus, but often to a highly complicated combination of stimuli. It is only the threshold of this particular stimulation that is raised, or in other words, it is only the response to this that decreases, while all other responses to all other stimulus situations, even for very similar ones, remain unaltered.

The second physiological property, also common to very many neural functions, is that of *inertia*. Any time lag in a regulative cycle leads to the effects of rebound and oscillation. If a deviation from the *Soll-Wert* is caused in any homoeostatic cycle, the restitution of this value is hardly ever reached in a direct dampened curve, but in most cases *overshoots* the reference value and only reaches it at last by way of one of several oscillations above and below the value. This overshooting of the mark set by the regulating system constitutes what is generally called a rebound or a contrast. Among other more complicated causes, contrast is one of the factors which makes activities appear in bursts or bouts, instead of "dribbling" constantly. In the constant presence of food, for example, an animal does not eat constantly and very slowly, but eats its fill and then stops for a considerable time. This is because the regulating cycles of food uptake overshoot the mark both ways: first the animal continues eating, by virtue of inertia, slightly longer than it ought to, then, having slightly overeaten, it remains refractory to the constantly present food, because the stimulation emanating from the latter, by "creeping in," elicits a response again slightly larger than would exactly correspond to the threshold of the reference value.

Lastly, in order to understand the function of the pleasure-displeasure-equilibrating apparatus, it is necessary to consider the circumstances under which it originated historically. At the time of its probable origin humanity eked out a precarious existence. Hence it bears the earmarks of a selection pressure working in the direction of the utmost economy. At the dawn of humanity, men could not afford to pay too high a price for anything. They *had* to be extremely reluctant to make any expenditure of any kind, of energy, of risk, or of possessions. Any possible gain had to be greedily seized upon. Laziness, gluttony, and some other present-day vices were virtues then. To shun everything disagreeable, like cold, danger, muscular exertion, and so on, was the most advisable thing they could do. Life was hard enough to exclude all danger of becoming too "soft." These were the circumstances to which our mechanism balancing pleasure and displeasure has been adapted in evolution. They must be kept in mind in order to understand its present miscarriage.

For obvious reasons, our apparatus of pleasure-displeasure economy is prone to dysfunction under the conditions of modern civilization. Man has been all too successful in evading and circumventing all stimulus situations causing displeasure, and all too clever in devising more and more rewarding "supernormal" enticements. The inevitable consequences of this has been an ever-increasing sensitization to all stimulation eliciting sensations of displeasure, accompanied by a corresponding waning of the responses to formerly pleasurable stimulus situations. It is an old, hackneyed truth that there is no joy, however great, which does not become stale with constant repetition, yet modern humanity seems to have forgotten it. Furthermore, in all his alleged wisdom, man does not seem to understand that the highest levels of happiness which are accessible to him at all can only be reached by exploiting the phenomenon of contrast. There is no path to the peaks of bliss except through the valley of sorrows, and modern man is so pampered and coddled that he shrinks from paying even the moderate toll of discomfiture and toil which nature has set as a price for all earthly joy. It is as simple as that!

To expend any joy down to the point of full exhaustion is outright bad pleasure economy and still worse, to push that point of heightened threshold still further up by finding supranormal stimulation. Such a procedure is comparable to driving a cart with a permanently tired horse which by continuous flogging cannot be made to go faster than a rested animal would go without the whip. Besides being unhealthy for the horse, this precludes a maximum performance which can occasionally be attained by whipping the well-rested horse. One should think that the stupidest human being on earth should see through that error, yet people don't. There are many sides to civilized life in which intelligent people commit faults analogous to that of a silly mother who thinks that she can increase the food intake of a weak child by feeding it exclusively on delicacies. In regard to the economy of pleasure, this is just as stupid as that which has frequently enough happened in commercial economy. The whaling industry, for instance, has exhausted the whale population to the point of leaving hardly anything worth exploiting and *keeps* it exhausted, because the exploiters lack the intelligence and foresight, as well as the financial reserves necessary for the only sensible strategy of letting the whale population recover to the extent at which it would furnish a maximum yield. This is a perfect commercial model of that which happens in human pleasure economy.

The inability to wait, to hold back for the period necessary to let the threshold of pleasurable stimulation recover their normal values, has, of course, pernicious consequences for the *rhythm* in which consummatory activities are repeated. As I have already explained, the apparatus which balances the price to be paid against the advantage to be gained is also responsible for the important function of making activities appear in bursts or bouts instead of "dribbling" continuously. This, however, is exactly what happens as the consequence of the disturbance here under discussion. The subject afflicted by it is unable to put up, even for a short period, with the slightest need. Like my young nephew, he may even be so afraid of the mildest pang of any want that he has to anticipate it even before he feels it. The normal rhythm of eating with enjoyment after having got really hungry, the enjoyment of any consummation after having strenuously striven for it, the joy in achieving success after toiling for it in near-despair, in short the whole glorious amplitude of the waves of human emotions, all that makes life worth living, is dampened down to a hardly perceptible oscillation between hardly perceptible tiny displeasures and pleasures. The result is an immeasurable *boredom*.

If you have eyes to see, you will perceive this boredom in a truly frightening multitude of young faces. Have you ever watched young people courting, kissing, petting, and all-but-copulating in public? You need not be a peeping Tom to do it, you cannot help observing if you walk in the evening through Hyde Park or ride on the Underground in London. In these unfortunates the fire of love and the thrill of sex are toned-down to the intensity of emotion to be observed in a pampered baby half-disgustedly sucking an unwanted lollipop. The bored juvenile is in a particular hell of his own, he must be an object of sincere pity, and we must not be deterred from our commiseration by the fact that he hates us more than anything in the world.

The causes of this hostility consist only partly in the disturbance of the pleasure principle of which I have spoken hitherto. To a greater part they lie in a dysfunction of the mechanism which transmits cultural norms of social behavior from one generation to the next. Of this I shall speak anon, but first I must discuss the arousal of hate by effects already mentioned.

The "going soft" is a rapidly progressive process, therefore the younger generation is automatically more severely afflicted by it than the older. Parents are therefore easily tempted to play the role of the "Spartan father" and to sermonize on the merits of a hard, frugal life. This, of course, is the worst thing they can do. The therapists who have successfully combated the phenomenon of *Verweichlichung* (the German word is the most descriptive by far, *pampering* or *coddling* seems to apply chiefly to the bringing-up of children and *effeminate* is a libel to women!) are unanimous in the opinion that the circumstances counteracting it must emanate from the impersonal environment and not from any human agency. Helmut Schulze, in his book *Der progressive domestizierte Mensch*, has pointed out some very interesting possibilities of therapy, and long before him Kurt Hahn had applied the same principle.

The nature of the therapy illuminates the primary root of the disturbance: the essence of all countermeasures consists in getting the "patient" into *real* trouble, which, if possible, concerns not only himself but is strongly evocative of social responses. The most effective therapy for "blasé" adolescents which Kurt Hahn could devise was setting them the task of saving life at some danger to their own. Helmut Schulze came to identical conclusions on the basis of the paradoxical observation that some of his patients who had lived in concentration camps and who had, under these dreadful circumstances, proved to be heroes of courage and altruism became neurotic or went to pieces in other ways as soon as they had regained the security of a soft, civilized life. Another illustration of the same paradox is furnished by the not infrequent cases of young people who find the softness of modern civilized life boring to the point of attempting suicide, succeed in hurting themselves badly, and afterward, amazingly, go on living happily with a broken back or with their optic nerves shot through. Now that they have a real trouble to face and conquer, they find life worth living.

To sum up: the cause of the symptoms hitherto discussed is, at least to a great part, to be found in the fact that the mechanisms equilibrating pleasure and displeasure are thrown off balance because civilized man *lacks obstacles* which force him to accept a healthy amount of painful, toilsome displeasure, or alternatively perish.

VIII. DISEQUILIBRATION OF MECHANISMS PRESERVING AND ADAPTING CULTURE

I now turn to the description of another set of symptoms, those which I believe to be caused by unbalancing of that system of behavior whose function it is to transmit tradition from one generation to the next, and, simultaneously, to eliminate obsolete and to acquire new and adaptive information. All these phenomena add up to a most alarming hostility which the younger generation bears the older and which is characteristically reciprocated only halfheartedly and only by a small proportion of the adults. A very small part of this hostility may be caused by the ill-advised attempt on the part of the older generation to act the part of the proverbial "Spartan father" in regard to the softening process already discussed. The young might forgive us our admonitions to take some exercise, they might even condone our earning the money on which they live. They hate us for other reasons and I am afraid they hate us very deeply indeed. It is not only the "rockers" who do so, though others do not go to the extremes of torturing people just because they are old. An ambivalent element of hate is noticeable to the initiated even in the behavior of sons who are overtly and consciously quite fond of their parents. Their hate is not *personal*, it is directed at *cultural* properties of the older generation. They hate our mode of life, our attitudes, the way we dress, wash, and shave, they distrust us and refuse to believe anything we say. They think that they are gloriously free from parental influence while in reality they are copying the preceding generation slavishly, if with a negative sign. When hippies wear elaborate velvet waistcoats and long, gloriously curling locks, skintight trousers, and chains round their necks, they don't do it because they really like it, but because *we dislike it*. All this is done to spite us, and the horrible thing is that we react exactly in the way we are expected to. At least I myself have to confess to a desire to kick the behinds of the languidly pretty young men and slightly less of the bearded, unwashed type. I am very angry with myself because I cannot prevent myself from getting angry, which is quite unworthy of the initiated ethologist—but there it is! Other old men, more dignified than I am and less prone to subject their own motives to a self-ridiculing ethological analysis, simply get uninhibitedly furious with the younger generation, and this mutual hostility, by a process of escalation, can reach dangerous levels wherever the younger and the older generation are thrust upon each other, as they are, for instance, at schools and universities.

The enmity which so many members of the younger generation bear the older has a lot in common with that which can be observed between two hostile ethnic groups. The term *ethnic group* is here meant to describe a very wide concept: that of any community whose individuals are kept together by their *regard for common symbols* rather than by personal friendship. The budding of an ethnic group begins with the first occurrence of *culturally ritualized norms of behavior* which are specific to the group. These ritualized norms may consist at first of quite inconspicuous mannerisms in an accent, in ways of dressing, and so on, as can be observed in schools, small military units, and similar small communities.

These group-specific ritualized norms play a most important part in keeping the group together. They are *valued* by all its members. "Good manners" are, of course, the manners of one's own group, its ways of dressing are those that are considered "elegant." Deviations from the rules set by these ritualizations are regarded as contemptible and *socially inferior*. Therefore, two comparable groups of this kind, each being aware of the contempt in which it is held by the other, will show a quick escalation of hostility. Hostile contact of this kind enhances the value which each group attributes to its specific ritualizations. Ethnologists have known for a long time that the etiquette and the old modes of peasant dresses which otherwise are rapidly disappearing all over Europe retain their traditional force in localities where different ethnic groups are in direct contact with each other, for instances in Hungary wherever Slovak and Hungarian villages are bordering on each other.

Ethnic groups developing independently of each other become more and more different with the lapse of time. In other words, their distinguishing properties permit deductions concerning their age and history much in the same way as the genetically fixed properties of animal and plant species permit the reconstruction of their genealogical tree. The *comparative* method is equally applicable in the elucidation of cultural and of phylogenetical history. Of course, one must be conversant with the subtleties and the pitfalls of this method, in particular one must know how to exclude convergent adaptation as a source of error. Of these methodological necessities, few ethnologists seem to be aware. Divergent cultural development erects *barriers* between ethnic groups in a manner very similar to that in which divergent evolution tends to separate species.

It was Erik Erikson who first drew attention to this phenomenon and coined for it the term of *cultural pseudospeciation*. In itself, it is a perfectly normal process and even a desirable one, because a certain degree of isolation from neighboring groups may well be advantageous to a quick cultural development, analogous to the reasons why geographical isolation facilitates the evolution of species. There is, however, a very serious negative side to it: pseudospeciation is the cause of *war*. The group cohesion effected by the common esteem of group-specific social norms and rites is inseparably combined with the contempt and even hate of the comparable, rivaling group. If the divergence of cultural development has gone far enough, it inevitably leads to the horrible consequence that one group does not regard the other as quite *human*. In many primitive languages the name of the own tribe is synonymous with that of Man—and from this viewpoint it is not really cannibalism if you eat the fallen warriors of the hostile tribe! Pseudospeciation suppresses the instinctive mechanisms normally preventing the killing of fellow members of the species while, diabolically, it does not inhibit intraspecific aggression in the least.

There is no doubt that the younger generation responds to the parent generation *of the same community* with all the typical patterns of hostile behavior which are normally elicited in the interaction with a *strange and hostile* group. Our deplorable familiarity with the phenomenon prevents us from realizing what a bizarre distortion of normal cultural behavior it really represents.

At this point let us ask Ronald Hargreaves's first question: What is the mechanism which we find disturbed and what is its normal function in the service of the survival of the species? Obviously, the functions concerned are those which normally ensure an ethnic group's continuance in time. I have already said that in the continued existence of a culture all those mechanisms which preserve and hand down from one generation to the next all the culturally ritualized rites and norms of social behavior are performing functions which are closely analogous to those which the mechanisms of inheritance perform in the preservation of a species. They *store* knowledge (*not* simple information in the sense of information theory) and pass it on from generation to generation. In my paper "Innate Bases of Learning" I explained what happens to a species or a culture when stored knowledge gets *lost,* and I shall try to sum up what I said there as concisely as I can. If details drop out of the genetic "blueprint" of the general, large-scale structure of an organism, the consequence is a malformation; if the loss concerns the microstructure of tissues, the result is very often a regression to an ontogenetically or phylogenetically *more primitive* type of structure. Between these two, all kinds of intermediates are possible. If the loss of knowledge goes so far that in the body of a multicellular organism some cells altogether "forget" that they are parts of an adult metazoan, they will naturally revert to the behavior of unicellular animals or of embryonic cells, in other words they will begin uninhibitedly to multiply by division. This is how a tumor originates and, for obvious reasons, its malignity is in direct proportion to the extent of the regression, to the *immaturity*—as pathologists call it—of its tissue.

If only in parentheses, I must here mention an old hypothesis of mine which contends that some of the phenomena under discussion have a *genetic* basis. In all these alarming symptoms I cannot help feeling a strong undercurrent of *infantilism*. Diligence, long-term striving for future goals, patient bearing up with hard labor, the courage to take the responsibility for calculated risk, and, above all, the faculty of compassion are all characteristic of the *adult*, in fact they are so uncharacteristic of children that, in them, we all are gladly ready to condone their absence.

We know from the work of Bolck and others that man owes some of his specifically human properties to what he has called "retardation," in terms of common biological parlance, to neoteny. In my contribution to Heberer's book on evolution, I myself have tried to show that this permanent retention of infantile characters in man has its parallel in many domesticated animals, also that one of these characters retained, infantile *curiosity*, has been one of the essential prerequisites for the genesis of man. I have a shrewd suspicion that mankind has to pay for this gift of heaven by incurring the danger that a further process of progressive self-domestication might procedure a type of man whose genetic constitution renders him incapable of full maturation and who, therefore, plays the same role in the context of human society that immature cells, by their infiltrating proliferation, play in the organization of the body. It is a nightmare to think that disintegration of society may be caused by the genetic disintegration of its elements, because education—which is our hope otherwise—would be powerless against it!

Still I believe that the bulk of the disintegration phenomena here under discussion are "only" cultural. A culture, however, is nothing but a living system and a highly complicated and vulnerable one at that! As I have already pointed out, its structure is, in many points, analogous to that of systems of less high integration. The blueprint of the program which in precultural systems is stored in the genome is contained, in the case of human culture, in all the ritualized norms of social behavior, in all the symbols on which the cohesion of a culture is dependent, in the logic of language, in adherence to certain values, in short in everything that is handed down in tradition from one generation to the next. While genetic knowledge is present in coded form in every single individual of a species so that, in the case of a catastrophe, one survivor is, in principle, in possession of all the knowledge necessary to build the species up again, cultural traditional knowledge depends on a far more extensive and more vulnerable repository. Cultural knowledge—and with it a whole culture—can be snuffed out in the interval from one generation to the next. The individuals who have foregone the traditional knowledge of the culture from which they stem very often behave in a manner analogous to that of tumor cells. Being unable to fend for themselves, they fall back on parasitism.

It cannot be my task here to convince readers of the fact that our culture is in immediate danger of extinction. I can refer them to the work of people like Kurt Hahn, Max Born, John Eccles, Paul Weiss, and many others. That a sudden collapse of culture has not happened in previous history is no legitimate reassurance. There is no more blatant untruth than Rabbi be Akkiba's alleged wisdom that everything that happens has happened before. Nothing has, and I am setting out to demonstrate that the sudden break in cultural tradition is threatening just *now*. With that I proceed to Hargreaves's second question, concerning the causes which effect a malfunction, or even the cessation of function, in the mechanism of passing on tradition.

I must begin by describing a few functional properties of this mechanism. Though human intelligence and inventiveness "enter into" its results, the growth of a human culture produces something that is not "man-made" in the sense a bridge or an airplane is. In my papers on phylogenetic and cultural ritualization, I have explained in detail why this is so. Like a forest, a culture needs a long time to grow, and like a forest, it can be annihilated in one short holocaust. Unlike a forest, however, it does not leave behind it fertile soil on which new plants can grow quickly, but a barren land devoid of all fertility. To believe that a culture can be "made," starting from scratch, by one generation of men, is one of the most dangerous errors, not only of juveniles, but of many adult anthropologists. As Karl Popper has pointed out, the total destruction of our world of culture, Popper's "third world," would set us back to the Paleolithic.

The ritualized norms of social behavior which are handed down by tradition represent a complicated supporting skeleton without which no culture could subsist. Like all other skeletal elements, those of culture can perform their function of *supporting* only at the price of *excluding* certain degrees of *freedom*. The worm can bend wherever it wants to, we can only bend a limb where a joint is provided. Any change of structure necessitates dismantling and rebuilding and a period of increased vulnerability intervening between these two processes. An illustration of this principle is the crustacean which has to cast off its skin-skeleton in order to grow a larger one. The human species is in possession of a very special mechanism providing the possibility of change in cultural structure. At the approach of puberty, young people begin to loosen their allegiance to the rites and social norms of behavior handed down to them by family tradition and, at the same time, to cast about searching for new ideals to pursue and new causes to embrace. This "molt" of traditional ideas and ideals is a period of true crisis in the ontogeny of man, it implies hazards quite as great as those threatening the newly-molted soft-shell crab.

It is at this phase of man's ontogeny that changes are wrought in the great inheritance of cultural tradition. The puberal "molt" is the open door through which new ideas gain entrance and become integrated into a structure which otherwise would be too rigid. The culture-preserving and, therewith, species-preserving function of this adapting mechanism presupposes a certain balance between the old traditions that are to be retained and adaptive changes which make it necessary to discard certain parts of traditional inheritance.

In my opinion it is certainly this mechanism which sifts and hands down tradition and whose disturbance creates all the symptoms just described. We can proceed to Hargreaves's second question concerning the nature of the disturbance before putting a third one: What are its causes?

The essence of the disturbance indubitably lies in the fact that the process of *identification* by which the younger generation normally accepts and makes its own the greatest part of the rites and norms of social behavior characteristic of the older, is seriously impeded or entirely obstructed. Excellent books have been written on this subject by Erik Erikson, Mitscherlich, and others, so I need not enlarge on it.

However, it must be emphasized that this failure to identify with the social norms of the parental culture is the direct cause of truly pathological phenomena. The urge to embrace some sort of cause, to pledge allegiance to some sort of ideal, in short to *belong* to some sort of human group, is as strong as that of any other instinct. Like any other creature which, under the imperative drive of an instinct, cannot find its adequate object, the deracinated adolescent searches for and invariably finds a *substitute object*. Here, the pathological dysfunction is particularly significant for the analysis of the underlying phylogenetically programmed mechanism. The diagram of the social situation for which the unrequited instinct is pining appears to be simple, as all those stimulus situations tend to be which form the goal of appetitive behavior. The adolescent must have at his disposal a group with which to identify, some simple rites and social norms to perform, and some sort of enemy group to release communal militant enthusiasm. If you have seen the psychologically excellent musical "West Side Story," you have a perfect illustration of how all the social virtues of courage, unselfishness, friendship, and loyalty reach the highest, most glorious peaks in a gang war, entirely devoid of any higher aims or values, in an absolutely senseless orgy of mutual killing.

Art representing these deplorable dysfunctions would not move us as deeply as it does if it did not strike a chord which is still responsive in most of us. The very simplicity, the almost diagrammatic character of the sketch constitutes an appeal to very deep layers of our souls, to neither more nor less than the phylogenetic program of tribal warfare. What we observe in practically all the juvenile groups which break with tradition and take a hostile attitude to the older generation is the more or less complete realization of this program. The Hamburg rockers who declare open war on older people represent the most clear-cut paradigm, but even the most emphatically nonviolent groups are constituted on essentially the same principles. All of them are constructed as surrogates to assuage the burning need of adolescents who, by the processes described, are deprived of a natural group whose causes they can embrace and for whose values they can fight.

Considering all this, we are, I think, justified in our assumption that it is quite particularly the failure of normal identification which causes the alarming breakdown of the mechanism whose important survival function lies in the sifting as well as in the handing-down of cultural tradition from one generation to the next.

We now come to the question: What are the causes contributing to erect an apparently unsurmountable obstacle to normal identification? We can name a number of them, but we cannot be sure that we know all of them.

Optimists who believe that men and women are reasonable beings tend to assume that rebellious youth are impelled by rational motives. There are indeed many good reasons to revolt against the older generation. It is perfectly true that practically all "establishments" on all sides of all curtains are committing unpardonable sins against humanity. I am not only speaking af actual cruelties, of political suppression of minorities, like the Czechoslovakians, or of the mass murder of innocent Indians by the Brazilians, but also of the deadly sins against the biology and ecology of mankind which are consistently being perpetrated by all the governments: of the exploitation, pollution, and final destruction of the biosphere in and on which we live, of the constantly increasing hustle of commercial competition which deprives man of the time in which to be human, and of similar phenomena of dehumanization. The youthful do indeed have good reasons to take issue at the goals to which the majority of the older generation is striving and I think that they do indeed recognize the intrinsic worthlessness of utilitarian aims.

There are several circumstances which tend to raise our hope that there is an element of intelligent rationality in the rebellion of youth. One is its ubiquity: the youthful protest against Stalinistic orthodoxy in Communist countries, against race discrimination in Berkeley, against the utilitarian and commercial "American way of life" all over the United States, against the antiquated tyranny of professors at German universities, and so on. Another reason for optimism is that never, as far as I know, have the youthful exerted their powers in the wrong direction, never have they demanded a more effective commercial system, better armament, or a more nationalistic attitude of their government. In other words, they seem to know—or at least feel—quite correctly what is wrong with the world. A third reason for assuming that there is a considerable rational element in the rebellion of youth is a very special one: rebelling students of biology are far more accessible to intelligent communication than are those of philosophy, philology, and (I am sorry to say) of sociology.

We do not know how great a part of the rebellion of youth is motivated by rational and intelligent considerations. I must confess that I am afraid it is only a very small part, even with those young people who profess—and honestly believe—that they are fighting for purely rational reasons. The main roots of the rebellion of youth are to be found in wholly irrational, ethological causes, as I hope to demonstrate. Many adults have found, to their cost, that it is useless to try reasoning with rebellious young people. In many countries, left-oriented professors have attempted, rather pathetically, to propitiate rebel students by making all possible concessions to their demands. As the German sociologist F. Tenbruck has pointed out, this endeavor led, in every single case, to a concentration of attack on the would-be peacemakers, who were insulted with particular rancor and actually booed in exactly the same manner as a bull who refuses to fight is boed in the corrida. Political opinions play no role at all: Herbert Marcuse, extreme Communist and advocate of completely scratching all tradition, was insulted by Cohn-Bendit and his young people, not because he held other opinions—which he did not—but because he was nearly seventy years old. Anyone familiar with ethological facts needs only to observe the hate-distorted faces of the more primitive type of rebel students in order to realize that they are not only unwilling, but quite unable to come to an understanding with their antagonists. In people wearing that kind of facial expression the hypothalamus is at the helm and the cortex completely inhibited. If a crowd of them approaches you, you have the choice of either to run or to fight, as your temperament and the situation may demand. In order to avoid bloodshed, a responsible man may be forced to do the first—and be accused of cowardice in consequence. If he sees fit to fight, he will be accused of brutality, so whatever he does will be considered wrong. Yet it seems nearly hopeless to argue, as it appears impossible to reach the cortex across the smoke screen of hypothalamic excitation. However, what else should an old man do who is neither a coward nor brutal?

However, we must face the sad and highly alarming fact that whatever the rebelling youthful *say* concerning their reasons for rejecting everything the older generation stands for, their actions prove to anybody with some knowledge of neuroses that their real motivation is to be sought in much deeper and more archaic disturbances. When rebelling students resort to defecating, urinating, and masturbating publicly in the lecture theaters of the university, as they have been known to do in Vienna, it becomes all too clear that this is not a reasoned protest against the war in Vietnam or against social injustice, but an entirely unconscious and deeply infantile revolt against all parental precepts in general, right down to those of early toilet training. This type of behavior can only be explained on the basis of a genuine regression causing the recrudescence of ontogenetic phases of earliest infancy, or, from the historical viewpoint, precultural states of affairs far below those of Paleolithic times. This alone is a sufficient reason to suspect strongly that the foundation of this type of neurosis is laid very early in life. The alarming fact is not that this type of mental illness does indeed occur, but its overt symptoms evidently pass unnoticed or at least unrebuked by intelligent and otherwise responsible young people.

We are safe in concluding that a large part of the factors which, by preventing normal cultural identification, cause hostility in the youthful, is strictly nonrational. We may divide these factors roughly into three groups. The first are those which enlarge the gap which is to be bridged between two generations, the second are those which impede the process which normally effect the bridging, the third and most interesting are those which make the present-day young people of different cultures more similar to each other than to their own parents.

The rapid change which the explosion of technology enforced by irresistible technocracy forces on human ecology and sociology has the unavoidable consequence that cultural norms of social behavior are becoming obsolete at an ever-increasing rate. In other words, the proportion between those traditional norms which are still valid and those which have become obsolete is changing, with increasing velocity, in the direction of the latter.

Thomas Mann, in his marvelous historical and psychoanalytical novel about Joseph and his brothers, has shown most convincingly how complete the identification of a son with his father could be, could *afford* to be in Biblical times, for the simple reason that the changes necessary to be effected between one generation and the next were negligibly small. I believe that humanity has just now reached the critical point at which the changes in social norms of behavior demanded within the time period between two generations has begun to exceed the capacity of the puberal adapting mechanisms. The ever-increasing gap between the social norms which circumstances dictate to each generation has suddenly attained a size which the powers of filial identification fail to bridge. From the point of the young, the parents are hypocrites and liars. In a rapid escalation of hostility, they are even now beginning to treat each other as enemy groups.

The discrepancy between the rapidity of ecological change which technological development forces on humanity, and the relative slowness of the adaptive change possible to traditional culture, would, all by itself, be a sufficient explanation for the breaking-off of tradition. There are, however, a number of further causes contributing to the same effect. The indispensable process of *identification* is severely hindered by the *lack of contact* between the generations. Lack of parent-child contact even during the first months can cause inconspicuous but lasting damage: we know, by the work of René Spitz, that it is in earliest infancy that the faculty to develop human contacts passes through its most critical period. It is one of the functions that are dangerously prone to *atrophy* if not thoroughly used. The horrible syndrome which Spitz has called "hospitalization" consists of an "autistic" unwillingness to form human contacts at all, accompanied by a complete cessation of exploratory behavior, as well as by a "negativistic" response to external stimulation in general. The child literally turns its back on the world, lying in its crib with its face turned to the wall. This awful effect can be caused by the seemingly innocuous change of personnel which takes place in most hospitals. The baby begins, at the age at which it becomes able to recognize persons, to form a personal bond to one of its nurses and is ready to enter into a near-normal child-mother relationship with her. When this bond is severed by the routine change of personnel, the infant will try to form a second attachment and, halfheartedly, a third or even a fourth, but finally it resigns itself to an autism which is in its external symptoms very similar to infantile schizophrenia—whatever that may be.

Mothering a baby is a full-time job. The silly baby games are the beginning of cultural education and very probably its most important part. I do not know the English equivalent of *"Bocki, bocki stoß"* or *"Hoppe, hoppe Reiter"*; *"Guck guck—Dada"* can, I think, be translated by "Peek-a-boo." Have you ever seen a baby's face light up when it has just grasped the *communicative* character of such a game and starts to join actively in it? If you have, you will have grasped the importance of this first establishment of mutual understanding on a cultural basis. Nowadays young mothers all too often have no time for this kind of nonsense; many of them would feel self-conscious in doing such a silly thing as gently butting a baby with her head or hiding behind a curtain and popping out again, crying "peek-a-boo." I think they are afraid of treating a small baby too anthropomorphically.

It may seem surprising to some, though it really is not, this early education is obviously indispensable. It represents the infant's first introduction to *ritualized forms of communication*, and it would seem that, if this is not effected at the correct sensitive phase of the child's ontogeny, permanent damage is done to the development of its faculty to communicate at all. In other words, we have to face the fact that the majority of present-day babies are slightly, but noticeably "hospitalized." They talk later and they become toilet-trained much later, as is witnessed by the huge, diaper-distorted behinds of quite big children. On the principle of distrusting anybody over thirty, their mothers flatly disbelieve me when I tell them the age at which my children were toilet-trained. Today's children are literally "uneducated," they do not "know the first things." How should they, as nobody takes the time to tell them? So the basis for later phenomena of de-humanization is laid down at an early age, by diminishing the readiness for contact and compassion as well as by dampening the natural curiosity of man.

I am aware that the precept that all young mothers should spend most or all of their time with their babies is one that cannot be followed. The scarcity of mother-child contact is a consequence of the scarcity of time, which, in turn, is caused by intraspecific competition and ultimately by crowding and other effects of overpopulation. The same fundamental evils have, with equally disastrous results, wrought profound changes in the sociological structure of the family. The pre-industrial family was lucky in respect to several prerequisites of the successful handing-down of tradition. The family worked together, striving for common aims intelligible to the children. These helped their father at his work and, doing so, not only learned his craft but also developed a healthy respect for his powers and abilities. Mutual help engendered not only respect, but love as well. Very little disciplining and certainly no thrashings were needed to impress the children with the superior position which the parents held in the social rank order of the group. Even the gradual taking-over of the leading position by the son was a frictionless, ritualized procedure which generated as little hostility as possible. Except in certain lucky, old-fashioned peasant families in some parts of Europe, I do not know where these happy circumstances prevail anymore. This is just too bad, because they are the indispensable prerequisites for the younger generation's readiness to accept the tradition of the older!

How many children of today ever see their father at work,

or help him in such a manner as to be impressed by the difficulty of what he is doing and his prowess in mastering it? Tired Pa, coming home from his office, is anything but impressive and if there is anything he wants to do less than talk about his work, it is to discipline a naughty child. He may even irritably shout at Ma when she—with full justification—thinks it necessary to do so. There is nothing to admire in her either, in fact she is the lowest-ranking creature within the child's horizon, because she is evidently rank-inferior to the charlady whose favor she is currying in an abjectly submissive manner for fear that this all-important person might give notice.

In addition to these hardly avoidable evils, the parents may have heard the "environmentalistic" theory that human aggression is only engendered by frustration and may try to spare their unlucky offspring the necessity of overcoming any kind of obstacle, including, of course, any kind of contradiction from their parents. The result is intolerably aggressive and, at the same time, neurotic children. Quite apart from the fact that trying to raise unfrustrated human beings is one of the most cruel deprivation experiments possible, it puts its unfortunate victim in a position of tormenting insecurity. Nobody, not even an all-loving saint, can ever *like* a nonfrustrated child, and the latter, with the great sensitivity which young children have for nonverbal expression, are very receptive to the suppressed hostility they arouse in every stranger with whom they come into contact. Defended by two despicable weaklings who do not even dare to slap back at a tiny child when slapped by it, and surrounded by a multitude of strangers who dearly would like to give them a sound thrashing, these children live in an agony of insecurity. Small wonder if their world breaks down and they become openly neurotic when they are suddenly exposed to the stress of public opinion, for instance on entering a college.

Young people are able to accept tradition only from a person or persons of the older generation whom they respect *and love*. It is as simple as that! When the family environment fails to produce these conditions, which very often coincides with a degree of early hospitalization, there is only a small chance that the adolescent may find a father figure in some other person, for instance in a teacher, with whom to identify himself. If this tenuous chance, too, is lost, the unlucky juvenile, in the phase of searching for new ideals, is completely at a loss, more than a little demoralized, and highly vulnerable to all the dangers of accepting an unworthy substitute object of his or her loyalty. From this, there are all possible gradations to outright neurosis.

A third set of factors which, while enhancing the cultural break between generations, might nevertheless prove beneficial in the end consists of all those which tend to minimize the differences between cultures. The mass media, the increasing facility of transportation, the all-embracing spread of fashion and other things all tend to make the representatives of the young generation more similar to each other than their parents had been, and indeed more similar to each other than to their widely divergent parents. Those that were reared after the last war were reared under circumstances and in an atmosphere entirely different from that of their parents' childhood. In this respect, their relation to their parents has been rightly compared to the one existing between the children of immigrants into a new country and these immigrants themselves. This, in fact, represents a silver lining in an otherwise very dark cloud: if the break of traditional knowledge is not so complete as to cast humanity back to a precultural state of affairs, one might cherish a faint hope that the youthful of the whole world, while waging war upon the older generation, might become less prone to do so on each other.

IX. CONCLUSIONS AND OUTLOOK

Our culture is in an unbelievably paradoxical situation. Here on the one hand, we have an established culture, assiduously committing suicide in seven different ways. First, there is the population increase which will soon suffocate, if not our species, still all that is really human about it. Second, the rat race of modern commercialism threatens, in a truly satanic, vicious cycle, to accelerate to the point of insanity. Third, man is progressively destroying nature, devastating the biotope in and on which he lives. Fourth, there is the progressive *Verweichlichung* of which I have spoken which is the death of human emotionality and, therewith, of all truly human relationships. Fifth, an imminent danger of genetic deterioration of mankind is due to the fact that common decency in every civilized community is at a negative survival premium. Sixth, and quickest, is nuclear warfare, yet I believe it is the least dangerous, because of its obviousness. Everybody understands the threat of the atom bomb, but who cares about disintegration of culture, genetic deterioration, and who will even believe that insecticides can endanger the world in which we live?

The powers that be flatly ignore all these dangers—except when soil erosion or other consequences of overexploitation become financially disturbing. Yet any man of average intelligence and tolerably good education cannot fail to see them. This irresponsibility of the responsible is due neither to their being stupid or immoral, but to their *indoctrination*. Indoctrination may be regarded as public danger number seven. Fundamentally identical with superstition, it is camouflaged under pseudoscientific terminology and grows apace with the absolute number of people that can be influenced by the so-called mass media. The function of all doctrine, as Philip Wylie puts it, is to explain everything. Where doctrine rules, all possibilities of truth are gone, and, with it, all hope for an intelligent consensus. Indoctrination is, I think, the very worst of humanity's deadly vices!

On the other side, there are the rebelling youthful. At least some of them, and the best among them, are gloriously free from indoctrination and commendably distrustful of all doctrines; also, they are yearning for a just cause for which to fight, for real obstacles to overcome. There is no dearth of dangers to humanity which must be fought and our attempt to save mankind meets with a number of great obstacles which ought to be quite sufficient to keep the most ebullient militant enthusiasm of the young happily occupied for a long time.

The youthful *say* that they want to save mankind. We may be convinced that they are honest about this, and I even believe that some of them even have a real understanding for the predicament of man. But do they, collectively, show any promise of ever accomplishing their great task?

At present, they are indulging in the archaically instinctive pleasure of tribal warfare. The instinct of militant enthusiasm is not a whit less seductive than that of sex, nor less stultifying. And hate is the most absolutely stultifying emotion of all, as it precludes all communication, all acceptance of that kind of information that might tend to abate it. This is why hate is "blind" and why it is so dangerously prone to escalate.

We must face the truly horrible fact that the hate which the young bear us is of the same nature as national or tribal hate. It bears all its earmarks, the haughtiness of only regarding the own party as quite human, the tendency to discredit and vilify the enemy ("Never trust a man over thirty"), the honest conviction that it is a moral duty to stamp out the enemy's culture as completely as possible, and so on, and so on. All these are attitudes and slogans which we know only too well as the tools of demagogues well-versed in the technique of siccing one nation against another.

Of course, there is a certain danger that the older generation might reply in kind, in other words that there might be an escalation of the enmity between the generations. It is a fact that the young revolutionaries are actively striving to be as revolting to the older generation as they possibly can contrive to be. I know a number of highly intelligent and altogether admirable old gentlemen who are neither hidebound nor etiquette-ridden, but who would find it absolutely impossible to take seriously what a man dressed up as a hippie or a communarde has to say. I myself confess I should find it difficult to listen to M. Cohn-Bendit in his pretty blue blouse, or to suffer having flowers heaved at me by flower power. I honestly feel I should be in greater sympathy with Papuans throwing spears at me, and all this in spite of the fact that I know about my own instinctive responses and do my very best to suppress them. Professionally disciplined not to bite back when being bitten by a subject of my studies, I still doubt that I could keep up my readiness to communicate with

APO students when fully hit in the face by a paint bag, as an 80-year-old colleague has recently been in my presence in Göttingen.

Yet I do not think that there is any danger of the old ever hating the young in the manner the young hate the old. We of the older generation are prevented from doing so by the most archaic of instinctive responses, by those of parental care. Among the rebelling young there are our own children or grandchildren, and we find it impossible to cease loving them, let alone to hate them. This creates a queerly unbalanced situation of being hated and quite unable to reciprocate hate, and it seems to be human nature to react to the conflict thus produced in a very specific and unexpected manner. If somebody we love dearly suddenly flies into an apparently justified rage against us, we automatically and subconsciously assume that we have inadvertently given good cause for that rage. In other words, we react by feeling *guilty*. Highly social animals, such as dogs and certain species of geese show an analogous response. When unexpectedly attacked by an otherwise friendly companion they act "as if" it were their own fault, or else a mistake. In other words, they "react by not reacting," submitting to the attack by simply ignoring it, whereupon the attacker regularly ceases to be aggressive. In terms of observable behavior, the human "guilt response" is strictly analogous, whatever the accompanying emotions may be. I am sure that part of the feeling of guilt which at present is weighing down many people of the older generation has its source in the paradoxical reaction just described and that this is particularly true of the almost masochistic attitude assumed by some university teachers toward the rebelling young.

To sum up: our culture is threatened with immediate destruction by a breaking-down of cultural tradition. This threat arises from the danger of what amounts to a tribal war between two successive generations. The causes of this war, from the viewpoint of the ethologist as well as from that of the psychiatrist, appear to lie in a mass neurosis of the worst kind.

This diagnosis, though matter-of-fact, is pessimistic only in appearance, because any neurosis can, in principle, be cured by raising its subconscious and unconscious causes above the threshold of consciousness. In respect to the neurotic war between the generations it should not be too difficult to do just that. It ought to be quite easy to make those among the rebelling students who are neither hopelessly indoctrinated nor stupid understand the few biological facts of which I could give some idea even in one short presentation. The young *have* already grasped the one fundamental fact that humanity is going to the dogs at a rapid rate if some vicious cycles like population growth, destruction of biotope, and accelerating commercial competition are not stopped and *soon* at that.

They still have to understand a few further truths. One is that even if their whole generation consisted of nothing but blessed geniuses, they could not build up a culture from scratch, but would be back at Neanderthal if they followed Marcuse's precepts of destroying all tradition: tradition is to a culture what the genome is to a species. Another fact they must comprehend is that they should not give way to hate. Hating the older generation prevents them from learning anything from it, and there is a lot to learn. It is hate that makes them so stupidly haughty, that creates in them that exasperating inverted "mother-knows-best attitude" which makes them impermeable to advice and renders them actually paranoiac because everything one tells them is automatically interpreted as an attempt to uphold the so-called establishment. (If one criticizes the establishment one is suspected to be a particularly insidious and clever supporter of it.) Finally they should come to understand in fairness that if we of the older generation on being hated don't reciprocate hate, this is not because we are guilt-ridden, having perpetrated nameless crimes against them but because, being their parents, we cannot help loving them.

I am admittedly an incurable optimist and I believe that the youthful can be made to understand all this and that, if they once have grasped the simple ethological facts underlying it, they will not only be able to save and retain everything worth preserving of our present-day culture, but that they might do more: they are, as I said, even today loosening their allegiance to their several established cultures and they are becoming increasingly similar to each other, independently of their provenience. Provided they do not, by jettisoning the accumulated knowledge of their culture, relapse to Neanderthal, provided they attain power when they attain maturity, provided they do not then forget their present aims, and provided they do not get caught, as they are all too likely to be, in the orthodoxy of some doctrine or other (it does not matter in the least which), they really might be successful in getting mankind out of the horrible mess it is in at present.

All these high hopes depend, of course, on education, and if I have seemed overly optimistic just now, I have occasion to counteract that impression at once. One of the ugliest facts in the social life of present-day humanity is that the decision concerning what to teach to the young and what to withhold from them still rests almost exclusively with those who are in power politically. What is to be taught to the youthful and what is to be withheld from them is therefore mainly dependent on what the politicians deem advisable in the interests of their own, short-lived political aims and not on any consideration of what will be necessary for the present-day young people to know when, a few years hence, they will have to shoulder the responsibility for the survival of mankind. The teaching of Charles Darwin's discoveries is still legally prohibited in the state of Indiana, a few miles from Chicago. Biology, and particularly ecology and ethnology, are regarded as subversive sciences in many parts; the teaching of biology in German middle schools has been cut down to a ridiculous minimum.

Furthermore, the technique of all teaching, particularly in the United States, is still founded on the assumption that the pseudodemocratic doctrine is absolutely true. This results in a purely utilitarian teaching which leaves entirely out of consideration the fact that man possesses certain species-specific programs of behavior, the suppression of which inevitably leads to neurosis and contributes to the horrible mass neurosis with which we are confronted nowadays. In other words, the usual kind of education intentionally or unintentionally ignores the fact that the realizations of certain phylogenetically evolved programs of human behavior constitute unalienable human *rights*. So far from being a mere quibble, the question whether a certain pattern of human social behavior is determined by a phylogenetically adapted program or by cultural ritualization becomes of supreme importance the very moment we have to deal with a pathological dysfunction. Its correction requires entirely different steps in each of the two cases. If the disturbance has its source in cultural tradition alone, education alone ought to be capable of dealing with it. If the central cause of the disturbance lies in a phyletic program which, by remaining unfulfilled, causes malaise and even neurosis, educative measures will only serve to make matters worse by destroying what faith in the educator is still left. One cannot *teach* a man to remain happy, to retain his love for his neighbor, to avoid developing neuroses, high tension, and heart attacks under the stressful conditions of crowded, commercial city life. Which is exactly what present-day education is persistently and unavailingly trying to do.

Even from the full recognition of the *cause* of certain pathological phenomena it does not follow that a means of combating them is automatically apparent. There are many examples in medical science demonstrating this sad fact. However, I believe that an increased emphasis on teaching biology, in particular ecology and ethology, on teaching young people to think in terms of systems rather than in those of atomism, together with a certain amount of tuition in pathology and psychopathology, would help enormously to make young people understand the real predicament of mankind. This considered opinion of mine is founded on what I regard as a highly suggestive fact. Among the rebelling students there is a clear positive correlation of their knowledge to biology and the constructiveness of their demands. The deepest malaise, the most uncompromising enmity against the teachers, the deepest confusion of the intentions of the teachers and those of the politicians in power, in short the greatest amount of general disorientation, is to be found among the students of sociology, a science which I reproach for being still too much under the influence of the pseudodemocratic doctrine. In a discussion of three hours' duration which I had late at night with APO students in the streets of Göttingen, a discussion which began in hostility and ended in friendship, I could not offer any better suggestions for the solution of the problems of education just mentioned than I have to offer now. Politicians can only be influenced by the pressure of public opinion. There is only one way to gain their attention for our problems, and that is by *infiltrating public opinion* with the knowledge of the real causes of man's predicament and trust the public to force politicians to do the right things. It is an error common among scientists to underrate the intelligence of the public, and that is why all too few scientists regard it as their duty to write generally intelligible books, leaving this task to popularizers who rarely accomplish it in a satisfactory manner. If science is ever to gain that kind of influence on politics which is obviously necessary to save mankind, it can only do so by educating the public independently of accepted political doctrines.

LOIS BARCLAY MURPHY

Infants' Play and Cognitive Development

Young mothers and preschool teachers are all familiar with the fact that children from three on up project in their free play activities the basic time-space patterns of their lives. Some time ago, I discovered to my astonishment that this principle does hold not only for children in Western civilization but also for children in India. These Indian children often set up a large circle of dolls, as if representing the extended family, much as children in the United States set up episodes from the nuclear family life familiar to them. From hundreds of observations of children on both the Asiatic and the North American continent I thus concluded that children develop the capacity to play out their particular time-space pattern quite naturally, just as they learn to walk.

Recently, though, I have been amazed to find how some extremely deprived children from disorganized, overcrowded ghetto apartments do not create these patterns. Not only do they lack vocabulary range and curiosity, as described by other observers; they do not play with words or materials as middle-class children typically do. They like to indulge in sensory play with sand, water, clay, and finger paints—and to wash a baby doll or make a sand pie; but they do not organize toys, or solve balance, weight, and space problems with blocks; nor do they achieve new integrations or impose new structures on materials of the environment until they have experienced the structure of the day care center itself for some time. The children from the most apathetic, disorganized families don't come into the day care center with an idea of building a garage or a fire station; much less do they integrate toys and children in a complex play pattern. At a macrocosmic level they may play at eating or getting whipped or other happenings but they do not project *sequences* which involve making a plan and carrying it out. (This does not gainsay their adroit survival skills, their ability to manipulate people to get what they want, and their capacity to catch the wandering toddler.) When we find extreme poverty children who do organize these structures, they are generally from the best functioning families of the neighborhood.

The lack of higher level structuring in deprived children led me to wonder about its precursors and prerequisites and about the nature of play. Play at the preschool stage is not primarily a survival skill. It is supposed to be fun, although at times in our sports-coercive culture it doesn't live up to this expectation, for fun stops when one *has* to play. For example, Colin, a couple of years after the end of the period covered in my book about him, was asked by his teacher one fine spring day, "Don't you want to go out with the other boys and play soccer?" He shook his head. "No. I want to sit here on the window sill and write a poem."

When, then, is play fun? It seems that play is most fun,

and most playful, when it is spontaneous, evolving from an integration of impulse and ideas and providing expression, release, sometimes climax, often mastery, with a degree of exhilaration, and refreshment. Good play leaves one feeling good, happy, alive. It is different from just passively watching TV. With children, play is psychically active, if and when the child is free to enjoy and to impose something, some structure, some pattern on the environment.

Where do these patterns come from? Where do children find them? Middle-class preschool children, merely encouraged to "do anything you want to" with the Miniature Life Toys, show us that these patterns are individually shaped by wishes, angers, fears, conflicts, worries—as play therapists have reported. But the patterns also reveal puzzlements, questions, a need to clarify experience, to make a cognitive map, or to improve on nature.

At the age of four, Jennie, whose mother and two aunts were all pregnant, placed a kitchen stove, a toilet, and a baby in a crib, as if asking, how do breakfast, and B.M.'s, and a baby manage inside mommy's tummy? Colin, puzzling over the baby girl's lack of a "tinkler" after his little sister was born, found a tiny piece of rubber and gave the doll-baby a tinkler. (Incidentally, at this juncture Colin has just finished his surgical internship.) Kurt, at three, arranged an oblong with all the furnishings of a house, then placed a little boy doll and a horse on a boat as if to go off on an adventure. He did this shortly after his mother had architected and furnished a new house, after which she took her small son off on a trip. Time sequences, as well as space representations such as these exemplify the kind of structuring which is absent in severely deprived children.

In searching for possible prerequisites for the capacity to

produce time-space patterns, prerequisites which might be missing in the experience of destitute children, I watched mothers with their babies in severe poverty groups and compared them with others in better circumstances. I also checked through the infant-with-mother records of Escalona and Leitch. The following examples are some of the earliest steps in play that I found: Middle-class mothers speak of the very young baby's play with the nipple, or with food. "He's just rolling it around with his tongue." "He's playing with his nipple"—that is, after hunger is satisfied and survival needs are met. As a baby rolls around his tongue, his lips and buccal surfaces no doubt provide a variety of interesting tactile sensations, while also contributing a richer cognitive awareness of the nipple and of his mouth. This may be the beginning of some perception of self.

The mother contributes further to the baby's perception of himself, and herself, by playfully fingering his hands and toes, stroking his legs and patting his back. All these actions provide sensations which gradually become organized into a cognitive map of himself, perhaps with the basic sense that "There is such a lot of me and all so luscious," as Whitman put it. Narcissism, the cognitive experience, and cathexis of the outside are all very closely interrelated in this first play. Soon, the infant also pats and pushes the arms and body of the mother. Thus, well before he is able to bang a rattle on his cradle-gym or swing at other objects which provide tactile, auditory, or visual feedback, he experiences his own impact on the environment. As soon as he learns that he can do something to an object, he goes on endlessly testing, trying new forms of contact, pushing, swiping at, feeling with his fingers, tasting and exploring with his lips and tongue.

In this earliest period, sequences of being done to and doing to are close together in the mini-acts with perhaps more than mini-pleasure. As he enjoys the contact with his mother, he gradually cathects the wider environment. The more feedback he gets, the greater is his investment and drive to explore and discover new experiences. Thus he develops "curiosity," which continues to lead him to new discoveries, perceptions, and concepts of the world around him.

After the first months, Mother's gentle tactile stimulation may be superseded by more active rocking and bouncing, and then by games such as peek-a-boo. This activity by the mother provides complex kinesthetic-tactile-visual-auditory experiences, which, in line with Piaget, we believe are internalized as patterns which the child to some degree remembers when at four or five months he bounces on mother's lap, thereby inviting her to play that bouncing game again. This new integrative step implies some notion of "let's play" and the cognitive anticipation that his relevant acts will evoke play with the mother.

It is precisely this active exchange of play signals—in cooperation with complex patterns and sequences—which the extremely deprived baby with a destitute, exhausted mother does not have any more than do babies in some foundling homes. The discouraged, apathetic mother just sits, passively holding the baby, without face-to-face communication, much less active playful mutual responses to the baby. The deprived baby does not have the experience which provides cognitive-motor-affective patterns for internalization to be later externalized; nor does he have the kind of experience which leads him to the realistic expectation that reaching out, exploring the outside, trying out new impacts upon it would bring pleasant results. He has less basis for conceiving of positive sequences.

And since many a poverty child's life patterns are also undependable, the time sequences fluid, and space disorganized, he cannot internalize clear structure. Thus the extremely deprived baby remains at a primitive level of development, exploiting sensory experiences and immediate gratification over and over again. He cannot externalize structure he has not internalized; he cannot create new patterns with his playthings, much less develop the capacity to sublimate. Thus he is deprived of turning passive experiences into active mastery and therefore fails to develop a sense of competence beyond elementary motor skill.

With apologies to Dr. Winnicott, we have to say that "holding" is not enough. It must be followed by increasingly complex interaction. The early impulse to make something happen in the environment must be reinforced by the experience that something actually does happen. In order to repeat his action, the baby needs the feedback which exhausted mothers frequently cannot supply. In severely deprived homes interplay is minimal. Even feeding and cleaning are done in a random fashion and rarely used playfully, all of which makes it hardly worthwhile for the poverty child to invest in the environment. What else does he miss? As Sally Provence has described, the healthy mother will play with her child from the sixth month on up games with a time-motion-vision sequence, such as pat-a-cake or peek-a-boo. These sequences, we assume, contribute to the invention of more complicated games. For at ten months or so the well-mothered baby initiates new patterns; he will, for instance, throw his teddy bear out of his high chair for mother to pick up. The sequence "I throw—you pick up—I throw—you pick up . . ." is often accompanied by triumphant crows. Evidently these increasingly complex patterns are the foundation for imposing structure on the environment, or to put it into everyday language, to be constructive. In Piaget's terms, assimilation is being followed by action patterns directed toward the object.

At about twelve months the well-developing child discovers a new pattern. It could be called "I do what you do to me." This includes not only the daily routine such as "I brush my hair" (as you brush my hair) and "I feed you with a spoon" (as you feed me with a spoon) but also more traumatic and painful events such as "I examine your ear" (as the doctor examined my aching ear). Thus, turning a passively endured experience into an active one helps the child to master the stressful experience.

At sixteen or eighteen months, when deprived of mother's presence, a child will be a mother to her doll, thereby not only compensating for the temporary loss of mother but clarifying her caretaking role while identifying with it.

Two- and three-year-old children discover yet another dimension of problem solving, by playing, for instance, "going to the hospital and getting into bed next to mother and her new baby." Such a game evokes some of the comforts of reality; and it also effects, through symbolization, a sense of reunion with her mother. The ability to turn longing into compensatory fantasy in order to cope with loss utilizes prior cognitive mastery, to which the mother's explanations probably contributed. Such explanations are also conspicuously lacking in the relationship between a very destitute mother and her baby, and so, therefore, is the compensatory fantasy.

By the age of three to four years, among well-mothered (not all), middle-class children—when autonomy and basic skills are sufficient for self-management and therefore separation from mother is possible—cognitive maps are produced with time-space patterns detached from the mother-baby relationship; the child may now re-create home or zoo or farm, or a sequence of activities going on in such settings without, however, being preoccupied with his relation to mother. The cognitive structure can be utilized for complex planful time-space organizations of unstructured materials available in the environment. He has mastered his world enough to re-create it—and then to use the constructive potential developed in infancy for problem solving, sublimation, and for creativity.

Why doesn't the maternally deprived child develop in this manner? After all, he too knows his way around. He too gets along without his mother. He manages for himself. But he did not experience and internalize the integrated organized sequences which occur in active play with mother. He remains at the primitive sensory or motor level of playing with water and sand, without goals, or running around without a purpose.

In order to become goal-oriented a child evidently needs the early experiences of efforts rewarded, evocative gestures and actions responded to, and support for reaching out, so he can begin to explore and to make his early cognitive map. Without this response, motility remains aimless or it merely serves primitive sensory experience. Moreover, the larger world does not beckon, and the potential for wonder and discovery is stunted. In short, it seems that not just elementary care, but active mutual mother-baby play is a prerequisite for the development of the cognitive structuring which can carry play beyond primitive sensory-motor stages to a goal-oriented symbolic and constructive stage. Moreover, the playful capacity underlying creativity is supported by good feelings as well—partly, I believe, because it evokes the joy, the delight, the fun of the earliest mother-baby duets.

ERIK H. ERIKSON

Play and Actuality

I

Maria Piers's benevolent planning has made me the last speaker in this series of symposia and permits me to do two things—one hardly dreamt of, the other habitual throughout my professional life. I never dreamt of having the last word after Konrad Lorenz, Jean Piaget, and René Spitz. And I welcome the opportunity after numerous digressions to turn once more to the play of children—an infinite resource of what is potential in man. I will begin, then, with the observation of one child's play and then turn to related phenomena throughout the course of life, reflecting throughout on what has been said in these symposia.

In the last few years Peggy Penn, Joan Erikson, and I have begun to collect play constructions of four- and five-year-old children of different backgrounds and in different settings, in a metropolitan school and in rural districts, in this country and abroad. Peggy Penn acts as the play hostess, inviting the children, one at a time, to leave their play group and to come to a room where a low table and a set of blocks and toys await them. Sitting on the floor with them, she asks each child to "build something" and to "tell a story" about it. Joan Erikson occupies a corner and records what is going on, while I, on occasion, replace her or (where the available space permits) sit in the background watching.

It is a common experience, and yet always astounding, that all but the most inhibited children go at such a task with a peculiar eagerness. After a brief period of orientation when the child may draw the observer into conversation, handle some toys exploratively, or scan the possibilities of the set of toys provided, there follows an absorption in the selection of toys, in the placement of blocks, and in the grouping of dolls, which soon seems to follow some imperative theme and some firm sense of style until the construction is suddenly declared finished. At that moment, there is often an expression on the child's face which seems to say that *this* is it—and it is good.

Let me present one such construction as my "text." I will give you all the details so that you may consider what to you appears to be the "key" to the whole performance. A black boy, five years of age, is a vigorous boy, probably the most athletically gifted child in his class, and apt to enter any room with the question "Where is the action?" He not only comes eagerly, but also builds immediately and decisively a high, symmetrical, and well-balanced *structure*. (See Fig. 1.) Only then does he scan the other toys and with quick, categorical moves, first places all the *toy vehicles* under and on the building. Then he groups all the *animals* together in a scene beside the building, with the snake in the center. After a pause, he chooses as his first *human doll* the black boy, whom he lays on the very top of the building. He then arranges a group of adults and children with outstretched arms (as if they reacted excitedly) next to the animal scene. Finally he puts the babies into some of the vehicles and places three men (the policeman, the doctor, and the old man) on top of them. That is it.

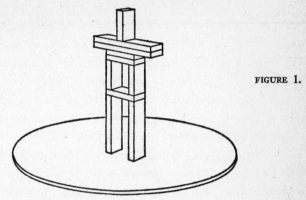

FIGURE 1.

The boy's "story" follows the sequence of placements: "Cars come to the house. The lion bites the snake, who wiggles his tail. The monkey and the kitten try to kill the snake. People came to watch. Little one (black boy) on roof is where smoke comes out."

The recorded sequence, the final scene as photographed, and the story noted down all lend themselves to a number of research interests. A reviewer interested in sex differences may note the way in which, say, vehicles and animals are used first, as is more common for boys; or he may recognize in the building of a high and façade-like structure something more common for urban boys. Another reviewer may point to the formal characteristics of the construction—which are, indeed, superior. The psychoanalyst will note aggressive and sexual themes not atypical for this age, such as those connected here with the suggestive snake. The clinician might wonder about the more bizarre element, added almost as a daring afterthought, that of men of authority (doctor, policeman, old man) being placed on top of the babies. Such unique terms, however, escape our comprehension in this kind of investigation, and this usually for lack of intimate life data.

In looking for a theme unique for this boy and unitary in its dominance, I would first focus on the block construction itself, "topped" as it is by a black boy. The meaning of this configuration emerged as we listened to Robert's teachers. One said, "Physically, this boy can compete with boys much older than he. But when he is unhappy, he becomes quite detached and dances a two-step around the classroom with his arms stretched out sideways." As the teacher mimicked his posture, the boy's structure revealed itself as a body image: legs, torso, outstretched arms, and head. Another teacher gave a second clue: she had once congratulated the boy on his athletic ability, but he had responded with a despairing gesture, saying, "Yes, but my brain is no good." She had assured him that body and brain can learn to help each other. This must have impressed him as a formula for the solution of whatever some inner conflict had come to mean to him, or his blackness, or his age, or all three. At any rate, the theme of a dancing body with a black boy as head literally stands out by priority, prominence, and centrality.

It would take a comparison of a wide variety of such constructions to make the probable meaning of this one construction convincing. Today we must accept this one performance as an example of a five-year-old's capacity to project a relevant personal theme on the *microcosm* of a play table. (1)

II

Our model situation, then, owes its relevance to the observation that one child after another will use a few toys and ten to twenty minutes' time to let some disturbing fact of his life, or some life task, become the basis for a performance characterized by a unique style of representation. Let me try to give some added dignity to the matter by merely mentioning that other play constructions done by the same child over a period of time show an impressive variation as well as a continuity of themes. And if I ever doubted that such continuity is a witness of unifying trends close to the core of a person's development, I learned better when quite recently I had an opportunity to compare the play constructions done in the manner just described thirty years ago by children in their early teens with the dominant themes in their subsequent lives.* History, of course, assigned unexpected roles to many of these persons who are now in their early forties; and yet many of these constructions decades later can be clearly seen as a condensed statement of a theme dominant in a person's destiny.

In studying such specimen, such condensed bits of life, the observer is loath to fit them into the theories to which he and others at different times and under other conditions have subordinated related phenomena. True, the themes presented betray some repetitiveness such as we recognize as the "working through" of a *traumatic* experience: but they also express a playful *renewal*. If they seem to be governed by some need to *communicate*, or even to *confess*, they certainly also seem to serve the joy of *self-expression*. If they seem dedicated to the *exercise* of growing faculties, they also seem to serve the *mastery* of a complex life situation. As I would not settle for any one of these explanations alone, I would not wish to do without any one of them.

* As recorded in the Institute of Human Development of the University of California.

Rather, I would now quote one of my predecessors in this symposium in order to underline one of the basic principles bequeathed by him to the Erikson Institute.* Declaring that he is an "interactionist," Piaget said: "What interests me is the creation of new things that are not preformed, nor predetermined by nervous system maturation alone, and not predetermined by the nature of the encounters with the environment, but are constructed within the individual himself." Piaget concluded by suggesting a liberating methodology in all teaching. "Children," he said, "should be able to do their own experimenting and their own research." Such experimenting, however (as I felt strongly when watching Baerbel Inhelder in Geneva induce children to be experimental), relies on some playfulness and, in fact, on an interplay of the child's inner resources with the nature of the task and the suggestiveness of interviewers who are "game." "In order for a child to understand something," Piaget concluded, "he must *construct it himself*, he must *re-invent* it."

Piaget, of course, spoke of cognitive gains. But let me suggest in passing that such play procedures as the one described may well facilitate in a child an impulse to recapitulate and, as it were, to re-invent his own experience in order to learn where it might lead. If there is something to this, then we may entertain the dim hope that some such play procedure may become an adjunct to early education rather than remain a method in the service of the clinic or of research only.

But what seems to be the *function of playfulness* in the children's responses both to Piaget's cognitive challenge and to

* Quotations from preceding symposia are taken from the original transcripts.

our expressive one? The most general answer necessarily points to a quality of all things alive, namely the restoration and creation of a *leeway of mastery* in a set of developments or circumstances. The German language has a word for it: *Spielraum*, which is not conveyed in a literal translation such as "playroom." The word connotes something common also for the "play" of mechanical things, namely *free movement* within *prescribed limits*. This at least establishes the boundaries of the phenomenon: where the freedom is gone, *or* the limits, play ends. Such a polarity also seems to adhere to the linguistic origins of the word *play*, which connotes both carefree oscillation and a quality of being engaged, committed. Language, furthermore, conveys any number of destructive and self-destructive nuances such as playing *at* something or *with* somebody, or playing oneself *out:* all these and other kinds of play connote the limits which end all play.

But if I should now make the first of a number of comparative leaps and ask where I would look for the closest analogy to our play constructions in adult life, I would point to the dramatist's job. If, in this small boy's life, the classroom and the home setting are an early equivalent of the sphere of adult actuality with its interplay of persons and institutions, then his solitary construction is the infantile model of the playwright's work: he, too, condenses into scenes of unitary place and time, marked by a "set" and populated by a cast, the tragic (and comic) dilemma of representative individuals caught in the role conflicts of their time.

III

Before turning to the sphere of human playfulness in later life, let me touch on some of its fundamentals in man's ontogenetic beginnings. Here I can point to René Spitz's discussion of "basic education." He, who has given us classical studies of the tragic consequences of a restriction of sensory *Spielraum* in early childhood, now has returned to specify what that deprivation consists of. He tells us that it is the gift of *vision* which first serves to integrate the "unconnected discreet stimulations" of taste, audition, smell, and touch. To him, the maternal person, visually comprehended, is both the earliest environment and the earliest educator, who "enables the child—all other things being equal—to achieve the capacity to learn." She seems to do so by truly letting her face shine upon the newborn's searching eyes, and by letting herself be thus verified as one "totality." I would prefer to speak of wholeness rather than of totality, in order to indicate the very special Gestalt quality of that visual integration which permits the infant to extend what I have called his *auto-sphere*, and to include the inclined human face and the maternal presence in it. As Joan Erikson puts it in her essay, "Eye to Eye": "We began life with this relatedness to eyes. . . . It is with the eyes that (maternal) concern and love are communicated, and distance and anger as well. Growing maturity does not alter this eye-centeredness, for all through life our visual intercourse with others is eye-focused: the eye that blesses and curses." (2)

Spitz now ascribes to organized vision the role of a first ego nucleus, anchored "in a special sector of man's central nervous system, which permits a first integration of experience." It will be obvious that a certain playfulness must endow visual scanning and rescanning, which leads to significant interplay as it is responded to by the mother with playful encouragement. This, in turn, confirms a sense of mutuality in both partners.

It is such *interplay*, I would believe, which is the prime facilitator of that "ego nucleus."

If these matters are reminiscent of religious images such as the inclined face of the Madonna and the aura of her oneness with the Christ child, I also believe that the phenomena which René Spitz (and Joan Erikson) refer to, *are* the ontogenetic basis of faith, a fact which remains both elemental and fateful in man's whole development. Let me illustrate this theme with an example from art history.

In our seminar on Life History and History at Harvard, Professor Helmut Wohl enlarged on some autobiographic notes left by Michelangelo. The great sculptor right after birth had been given a wet nurse because his mother was too sick to take care of him. To farm an infant out to wet nurses was, it seems not atypical in the lives of men and women of that time; in fact, the patron of our meeting, St. Loyola, was brought up by a blacksmith's wife. The "other woman" in Michelangelo's case was the daughter and wife of stonemasons; and his first environment, being adjacent to a stone quarry in Settignano, must have had an inescapable auditory quality. At any rate, Michelangelo acknowledged that while his mother had given him life itself, the wet nurse ("perhaps joking or perhaps in earnest") gave him "delight in the chisel, for it is well known that the nurse's milk has such power in us . . . by changing the temperature of the body." (3) That chisel eventually (and under the protectorate of a fatherly patron, Lorenzo de' Medici) became for him the executive tool of his very identity. When he created young David, Michelangelo equated "David with the sling" and "I with the chisel." (4)

But if Michelangelo had two mothers, he, alas, lost both

early. He was separated from the wet nurse when he returned to his mother and then his mother died when he was six years old. Wohl presented to us the sequence of Madonna images that Michelangelo sketched, painted, or sculptured, the first in his late teen and the last in his late eighties. His Madonnas always show a marked distance between mother and child, beyond the Renaissance theme of the willful boy Jesus straining away from his mother's arms: here the Madonna herself is looking away from her child, her eyes remaining inward, distant and almost sightless. Only the very last of Michelangelo's preserved sketches of the Madonna portrays, in Wohl's word, a nearly "conflictless" image of mother and child. The Madonna holds the child close to her face and he turns to her fully, attempting to embrace her with his small arms. So it took the closeness of death for Michelangelo to recover what he had lost early in life, and one cannot help connecting this, the old man's refound hope, with Saint Paul's saying, "For now we see through a glass darkly: but then face to face: now I know in part; but then shall I know even as also I am known." (5)

This, of course, would seem to be only a subsidiary theme in Michelangelo's gigantic confrontations. He not only hammered away at his strangely tortured sculptures, sovereignly transcended by irate Moses; he also painted his own vision of Adam and the Creator and of Christ at the Last Judgment in the Sistine Chapel. In a sonnet, he describes how, at the crippling expense of his whole physique, he gazed up at the ceiling, lifting arm and brush: "my beard toward Heaven, I feel the back of my brain upon my neck." (6) But whether or not a mighty compensatory force intensified Michelangelo's creative furor, we may well pause to wonder at the very fact of the singular fascination which these artistically created visual worlds painted on hallowed halls hold for us. Could all this be ontologically related to the singular importance of that playfully structured visual field in the beginnings of childhood?

As we proceed, I will refer to other visualized spheres endowed with a special aura. I already have mentioned the theater. The dictionary says that the root of the word is *thea*—a sight, which, in turn, is related to *thauma*—that which compels the gaze. Maybe, the "legitimate" theater is only a special case, a condensed version of all the imagined, depicted, and theorized spheres (yes, there is *thea* in *theory*, too) by which we attempt to create coherencies and continuities in the complexity and affectivity of existence.* And we will not forget that the late Bertram Lewin spoke of a "dream screen" on which we experience our nightly visions.

IV

But I must now ask a theoretical and terminological question. If, as we are apt to say, the maternal caretaker is the

---

* I owe to Gerald Holton a number of suggestive references to Einstein's meditations on the nature of his mathematical inspiration. It is said that Einstein was not yet able to speak when he was three years old. He preferred communing with building blocks and jigsaw pieces. Later (in 1945) he wrote to Jacques Hadamard: "Taken from a psychological viewpoint, this combinatory play seems to be the essential feature in productive thought—before there is any connection with logical construction in words or other kinds of signs which can be communicated to others." (7) And, again: "Man seeks to form for himself, in whatever manner is suitable for him, a simplified and lucid image of the world (*Bild der Welt*),

first "object" playfully engaged by the scanning eyes, who are the "objects" in later stages, up to St. Paul's finite recognition? Are they, as some of us would be all too ready to say, "mother substitutes"?

First a word about the term *object*. Within a theory of cognition it makes sense to speak of object constancy as the goal of the newborn child's gradual comprehension of the coherence and the continuity of what he perceives. It makes sense within a theory of sexual energy called libido to speak of a growing capacity to "cathex" the image of a comprehensively perceived person and thus to become able to love. And it makes sense to describe with clinical shorthand as "object loss" the various deficiencies or regressions which make it impossible for a person to maintain either a cognitive sense of another person's wholeness, or the capacity to wholly love and accept the love of other persons. All this describes the conditions for, but it neither explains nor guarantees that interplay by which the growing person and those attending him are capable of maintaining and expanding the mutuality of "basic education." *

---

and so to overcome the world of experience by striving to replace it to some extent by this image. That is what the painter does, and the poet, the speculative philosopher, the natural scientist, each in his own way. Into this image and its formation he places the center of gravity of his emotional life, in order to attain the peace and serenity that he cannot find within the narrow confines of swirling personal experience." (8)

* The questioning of terms easily becomes part of a wider concern about conceptual habituation. What we have now heard of the importance of vision, must make us wonder to what extent the "classical" psychoanalytic technique itself may have helped to shape some of our concepts. For if vision is, indeed, the basic organizer of the sensory universe and if the beholding of one person's face by another is the first basis of a sense of mutuality, then the classical psychoanalytic treatment situation is an exquisite

Today, I think we would agree on three points. Cognitively seen, the first *object wholeness* experienced by the infant must somehow coincide with the first *subject wholeness*. This means that the coherence and the continuity of the object world is a condition for the coherence and continuity of the "I" as observer. This joint sense of being both subject and object becomes the root of a sense of identity.

Secondly, if for its very "basic education" the child depended on a mothering supported by a family and a community, so will it, all through life, depend on *equivalents* (and not on *substitutes*) of the constituents of that early mutuality. I would emphatically agree with Peter Wolff that on each stage of development a child is "identified by the totality of operations he is capable of"; and I would conclude that the early mother's equivalent in each later stage must always be the sum of all the persons and institutions which are significant for his wholeness in an expanding arena of interplay. As the radius of physical reach and of cognitive comprehension, of libidinal attachment and of responsible action—as all these expand, there will, of course, always be persons who are substitutes for the original mother. But that, as we know, can be a hindrance as well as a help, unless they themselves become part of that wider sphere of interaction which is essential for the increasing scope of what once was basic education. In our

---

deprivation experiment. It may be the genius of this clinical invention that it systematically provokes the patient's "free" verbal associations at the expense of a visual word, which, in turn, invites the rushing in of old images seeking a healing mutuality with the therapist. But sooner or later every field must become aware of the extent to which its principal procedure codetermines the assumed nature of the observed and the terms decreed most appropriate to conceptualize that nature.

five-year-old's play construction we saw reflected, in addition to impulses, fantasies and familial themes, the teacher and the school environment in the widest sense of an encounter with what can be learned. But so will, in adolescence, the peer generation and the ideological universe become part of the arena which is the equivalent of the early mother. In adulthood the work world and all the institutions which comprise the procreative and productive actuality are part of the arena within which a person must have scope and leeway or suffer severely in his ego-functioning. Thus on each step what had been "in part" will now be recognized and interacted with in its wholeness, even as the person comes to feel recognized as an actor with a circumscribed identity within a life plan. In fact, unless his gifts and his society have on each step provided the adult with a semblance of an arena of free interplay, no man can hope to reach the potential maturity of (presenile) old age when, indeed, only the wholeness of existence bounded by death can, on occasion, dimly recall to him the quality of that earliest sensory matrix.

V

What we so far have vaguely called interplay can be made more specific by linking it with the problem of ritualization which was discussed on the last occasion when Konrad Lorenz and I served together on a symposium. (9) His subject then was the ontogeny of ritualization in animals, and mine, that in man. Julian Huxley, the chairman of that symposium, had years ago described as ritualization in animals such instinctive performances as the exuberant greeting ceremonials of bird couples, who, after a lengthy separation, must reassure each other that they not only belong to the same species but also to the same nest. This is a "bonding" procedure which, Huxley suggested, functions so as to *exclude ambiguity* and to facilitate unimpaired *instinctive* interplay. Lorenz, in turn, concentrated on the ritualizations by which some animals of the same species given to fighting matches make peace before they seriously harm each other. It was my task to point to the ontogeny of analogous phenomena in man. But with us, so I suggested, ritualization also has the burden of *overcoming ambivalence* in situations which have strong *instinctual* components (that is, drives not limited to "natural" survival), as is true for all important encounters in man's life. Thus the ontologically earliest ritualizations in man, the greeting of mother and baby adds to the minimum facial stimulation required to attract a baby's fascination (and eventually his smile) such motions, sounds, words, and smells as are characteristic of the culture, the class, and the family, as well as of the mothering person.

Konrad Lorenz, the foster mother of the goose child, Martina, has rightly gained fame for his ability to greet animals as well as humans in a bonding manner. In the present symposium you had the opportunity of seeing and hearing him demonstrate the lost-and-found game, which in German is called guck-guck da-da and in English, peek-a-boo. Let me call all these and similar phenomena in man *ritualized interplay*. This extends from the simplest habitual interaction to elaborate games, and, finally, to ornate rituals.* Today when

* It specifically excludes, of course, the symptomatic "rituals" of isolated neurotics, as well as all derisive uses of the word *ritualization* as synonymous with repetitiveness and rigidification. All these, in fact, connote symptoms of deritualizations in our sense.

so many ritualizations so rapidly lose their convincing power, it is especially important to remember that in this whole area of ritualized interplay the most horrible dread can live right next to the most reassuring playfulness. Little Martina was running and falling all over herself for dear survival when she pursued Konrad Lorenz, and any accidental interruption of the ritualized behavior by which animals do away with ambiguity, can lead to murder. As to man, we only need to visualize again small children who cannot smile, or old persons who have lost all faith, to comprehend both the singular power and the vulnerability of ritualized reassurance in the human situation.

Yet, what constitutes or what limits playful ritualization in man is as hard to define as play itself: maybe such phenomena as playfulness or youthfulness or aliveness are defined by the very fact that they cannot be wholly defined. There is a reconciliation of the irreconcilable in all ritualizations, from the meeting of lovers to all manner of get-togethers, in which there is a sense of choice and ease and yet also one of driving necessity: of a highly personalized and yet also a traditional pattern; of improvisation in all formalization; of surprise in the very reassurance of familiarity; and of some leeway for innovation in what must be repeated over and over again. Only these and other polarities assure that *mutual fusion* of the participants and yet also a simultaneous *gain in distinctiveness* for each.

Before moving on to adolescence, let me stop, in passing, to recount an experience which illustrates the relevance of all this for the school age. We recently visited a Headstart School in Mississippi, in an area where sniping nightriders and arson were then still expectable occurrences whenever Blacks consolidated a new kind of community life with outside help. As visitors, we were called up to concentrate on how and by whom the children were taught and what they were learning. But we were equally struck by how these people had ritualized both "school" and "learning." With our academic eyes it was, in fact, not quite easy to know to what extent they were playing at being a school or actually were one. Obviously the arrangements for learning and singing together, but also those for eating and conversing constituted new roles under new conditions: to grow into the spirit of these roles seemed to be the heart of the matter. This, then, was ritualized interplay in the making; and only the whole milieu, the whole combination of building and equipment and of teaching mothers and of motherly teachers, of learning children and of helpful fathers and neighbors were a collective guarantee of the survival of what was being learned—whether, at this beginning, it was much or little. We could not help thinking of other schools, more easily certified on the basis of grim accomplishment where much is learned by inexorable method but often with little spirit. And yet, the final assimilation of what has been learned would always seem to depend on any "school's" cultural coherence with a growing environment.

The life of all schooling depends on all this; but so does the fate of the children who soon will enter the stage of adolescence—the stage when the young themselves must begin to offer each other traditional ritualizations in the form of spontaneous improvisations and of games—and this often on the borderline of what adults would consider the license of youth: will they then have learned to be playful and to anticipate some leeway of personal and social development?

VI

Children cannot be said or judged to be "acting" in a systematic and irreversible way, even though they may, on occasion, display a sense of responsibility and a comprehension of adult responsibility which astonishes us. Young people, on the other hand (as we realize in our time more than ever before), are apt to continue to play and to play-act in ways which may suddenly prove to have been irreversible action—even action of a kind which endangers safety, violates legality, and, all too often, forfeits the actor's future. And, in recent years, youth closer to adulthood has begun on a large scale to usurp responsibility and even revolutionary status in the arena of public action. This has resulted in lasting consequences even where the action itself may not have been much more than a dare or a prank on a stage of imagined power. Never before, then, has it been more important to understand what is happening in that wide area where juvenile play-acting and historical action meet.

The return in adolescence of childlike and childish behavior in the midst of an increasing anticipation of and participation in adulthood has been treated in innumerable textbooks. They point to the impulsivity of sexual maturation and of the power of the aggressive equipment and yet also to the vastly expanded cognitive horizon. There is the intensity of peer-group involvement at all costs, a search for inspiration (now often forfeited to drugs), and yet also the desperate need (yes, an ego need) for an ideologically unified universe sanctioned by leaders who would make both freedom and discipline mean-

ingful. To all this, I have added the discussion of identity—
and of fidelity. In my book such postadolescent "virtue" is
meant to represent a minimum evolutionary requirement
rather than a maximized ideal.* Actually the formulation of
such successive virtues was intended to follow the clinical
formula (quoted in Konrad Lorenz's paper) of our lamented
friend Donald Hargreaves: "What is the normal survival
function of the process here disturbed?" In other words, I
have emphasized fidelity because I think I have observed the
fateful deficit in ego-strength resulting from the absence of
such commitments as would permit youth to anchor its readiness for loyalty in social reality; and the equally fateful deficit
in meaningful social interplay resulting from a state of society
in which old fidelities are being eroded. I would, therefore,
follow Konrad Lorenz in asserting that all through man's
socio-genetic development, rites and rituals have attempted to
attract and to invest that fidelity. Where and when both generations can participate in them with affective and cognitive
commitment, these rites, indeed, are performing "functions
analogous to those which the mechanisms of inheritance perform in the preservation of the species." Today, as we all
agree, a deep and worldwide disturbance exists in this central
area of ritualized interplay between the generations.

But let me again take recourse in an observation which
every reader can match with variations from his own experience. A few years ago I was invited to attend a confrontation

* I must repeat this in view of such well-meant pictorial presentations of my
stages of life as that of the Sunday *Times* of New York, where the successive virtues were posed by models who, indeed, look "virtuous" in a class-
determined and even racist way: blond and blue-eyed, healthy and well-
kempt, and obviously brought up on mental health food.

between the trustees and the students of a great university which, months before, had been one of the first to undergo what for a while became obligatory crises on a number of campuses: occupation of the administration's citadel and "liberation" of captive documents; brutally effective police intervention followed by a rapidly spreading student strike; a confused arousal of the faculty; and finally a widespread bewilderment and depression on the part of almost all concerned, including the most learned and the most politically adept minds.

At this meeting there were old and wealthy men, the trustees; there were learned men and guests like me; there were some students (however selected); and there were specialists in group meetings who lent a certain technical expertise to what could have been a natural mixture of reticence and spontaneous confrontation. After a few days of plenary speeches and more or less strained small group discussions, the students decided to present their case in their own way and to confront the trustees with an improvisation. The setting was a kind of amphitheater. One young man with long blond hair played a leading part; he had the words *Jesus Saves* printed in strong colors on his sweat shirt. He exhorted the elders to "give in gracefully" to certain nonnegotiable demands. Another young man, having embraced the first in brotherliness, took him by the arm and led him, one by one, before some of the men of the Establishment. Pointing to the flaming motto on his friend's sweat shirt, he asked these men whether the inscription meant anything to them—and what had they done recently for their neighbors? Now, there are probably few groups of men who (in the light of their community's standards of charity) have done more for their "neighbors," both openly or privately, than have some trustees of our colleges. But, of course, the students had intended to confront them with their sins against the university's actual neighbors in the poor housing areas surrounding the campus and owned by the university. And they made it clear that they did not expect answers other than confessions of guilt. The old men, in turn, tried desperately to understand, because that was what they had come for. The situation became extremely tense, some students themselves (as they said later) beginning to feel like "freaks." Some faculty and some visitors began to show bitter annoyance.

A scene such as this leaves the viewer in doubt as to whether he is witnessing a theatrical improvisation, a mocking demonstration, or, indeed, an act of religious ritualization. To me, it was all of this and I said so: there were ceremonial fragments assembled in a manner half-mocking and half-deadly serious, flaunting as well as protesting such themes as brotherly love, charity, and sacrifice. But what had kept the performance from coming off was a failure of ethical nerve: the students had, with total righteousness, demanded that everyone should admit his sins except themselves, thus using Jesus to mock the elders: a mere turnabout of punitiveness, however, could never lead to a meaningful covenant.

I saw in this act (even/and) just where it failed, a combination of themes for which our time must find new forms, whether or not the leaders and organizers of such events consciously intend such renewal. The students, in fact, had succeeded (at the price of taking chances with their own credibility) to elucidate an overweening problem: they had played with a ritual fire which youth alone cannot possibly contain in a new universal form, and which in changing times can emerge only from a joint adulthood willing to take chances with new roles and that means: to play where it counts.

VII

Let me now turn to a historical example. One of the most noteworthy revolutionary ritualizations of recent times has been the founding of the Black Panther Party—noteworthy in our context as an illustration of youthful political imagination on the very border of disaster. Such ritualization can go to the core of history, whether it "succeeds" or not: it is successful if it makes an unforgettable point and if it has the flexibility to go on from there.

Much of the Panther's history has happened in the dark of the ghetto as well as in that legal twilight which confuses and scares the "law-abiding." Yet, there is no denial of a certain genius in the translation of values which Huey P. Newton (he was twenty-two years old at the time) and Bobby Seale displayed when they cast themselves and other young Blacks in totally new roles, and this at a time when black youth in this country needed new images of dignity and of heroism. The fact that this new image included gun-carrying in public seemed revolting to many, while it is, in fact, a traditional historical stance in formerly exploited and belittled minorities: the autonomous man with his own gun, a man ready to use it both as a symbol and as a weapon for the defense of his and his people's dignity—this stance has been true of the first American revolutionaries as well as in the radically different contexts of the modern Jews and the Diaspora,* and the erst-

* Eldridge Cleaver at one time acknowledged this parallel by saying that "psychologically" black people in America had "precisely the same outlook" as Eastern European Jews had under Theodor Herzl (*New Outlook*, December 1970).

while British Indians, all youths whom successful revolutions are apt to forget. Sometimes, there is a book involved as well as a gun: a book which testifies both to tradition and to the power of literacy. In Newton's case, it was a law book such as that found on the street on the night in Oakland when a policeman (himself only twenty-three years old) lost his life in a scuffle never clearly reconstructed. Newton survived and prevailed through years of solitary confinement with a healthy body and with undaunted stature. The image he created was based on the usurpation of the black American of the oldest right of all (other) Americans (a right engraved on the imaginations of our young and the young abroad by way of Western movies), namely to bear arms in the creation of a semblance of legality in an area not yet defined in its traditionalities.

Originally young Newton not only insisted on the traditional legality of the arming of citizens, but also attempted to sanction it with a new uniform and a discipline which, I think, even Gandhi might have acknowledged (if with some sadness) as a necessary step toward a nonviolent approach—necessary for the simple reason that he who would not know how to use a gun both well and with restraint would not know how and when not to use it. But Newton, in addition to protesting dramatically the negative identity of his own people as the meek and helpless victims of the lynch law and its daily ramifications, established as the enemy of his people the very uniformed men who had become to them representatives of a lawless law employed to protect usurped privilege rather than legality and to punish powerlessness as much as illegality. Thus he attempted to turn the very image of the protectors of such law into a negative identity, namely that of victimizers of the poor. The Black Panthers, then, are of interest precisely because, according to Newton's intent, this original "violence" was to be contained in a new code of discipline.

Revolutionary activity, however, is always beset with the dilemma of defining who and what is the law, and what disruptive act, when, and where, is political rather than criminal. There may be also the proud and mocking creation of a new "species," as attested to by the very party name, which, in the case of the Panthers, is that of an animal said to be ferocious primarily in defense, and the relentless and publicist verbal weapon of calling men of the "legitimate" police force "pigs." Such debasement of the opponent is a moral violence which arouses not only murderous hate in the defamed, it can also become a retrogressive stance in the defamer. In the American Black, of course, such defamation is grounded more than in any other social group, both in a common history of daily and total defenselessness (or what Newton refers to as the "truly oppressed") and in an explosive folk language long the only outlet for in-turned aggression—and in fact used with mocking as well as murderous abandon against other Blacks. The original imagery of the young leaders of the Black Panther movement (and I am talking about these origins of the movement and not about the tedious stance of its propagandistic habituation) surely contained, therefore, the possibility of creating a new set of roles, which often may have appeared to be all too grandiosely staged, but which did link past and future by recapitulating historical images in a radically new setting. True, certain titles of command seemed rather florid in the absence of an assured body of followers; but it must be remembered that revolutionary language—at total risk to itself—always challenges history to confirm what has already been claimed as certain. This is, of course, compounded where the revolutionaries are young, for youth and revolution both play with that theater of action where personal conversion and radical rejuvenation confirm each other, to the point that history's agreement is taken for granted. And sometimes, history assents. Our black revolutionaries differ from others in that they are not rebelling against a father generation. Their symbol of the Establishment is "the man"; yet, both examples given remind us to look for the adult counterplayers in attempted ritualizations demanding new kinds of generational transfer. And there we often find glaring vacancies in the cast required for the fulfillment of the script—vacancies impossible to fill by excitable police or by uncomfortable judges.

VIII

This is the "gap," then; Konrad Lorenz would convince us that it exists not only because of a combination of historical and technological changes, but because of a misdevelopment of evolutionary proportions. He reminds us of the pseudo-tribal character of much of the present-day rebellion; and to him the widespread and truly "bizarre distortions of cultural behavior" represent a new "infantilism" and a regression to a primitivity which he considers analogous to a "disturbance of the genetic blueprint." Looking at revolutionary youth from the point of view of an evolutionary ethologist, apparently he feels that humanity has reached a critical point when the changes in social norms necessary within the period between generations have begun to "exceed the capacity of the pubertal adapting mechanisms."

Lorenz introduces into the discussion a term which I used at the London symposium where I drew attention to the phenomenon of cultural pseudospeciation—meaning the tendency of human groups to behave as if they were *the* chosen species. Lorenz discusses the matter vividly:

> In itself, it is a perfectly normal process and even a desirable one. . . . there is, however, a very serious negative side to it: pseudo-speciation is the cause of war. . . . If the divergence of cultural development has gone far enough, it inevitably leads to the horrible consequence that one group does not regard the other as quite human. In many primitive languages, the name of the tribe is synonymous with that of man—and from this point of view it is not really cannibalism if you eat the fallen warriors of the hostile tribe! Pseudo-speciation suppresses the instinctive mechanisms normally preventing the killing of fellow members of the species while, diabolically, it does not inhibit intra-specific aggression in the least.

Before coming to the implications of pseudospeciation for youth and adulthood, however, let me ask what importance it may have for the problem of play. In the animal world, obviously the play of the young is linked with the adaptation of the species to a section of the natural environment. The play of the human child, however, must orient him within the possibilities and the boundaries first of what is imaginable and possible, and then to what is most effective and most permissible in a cultural setting. One of the playing child's tasks, then, is to try out some role pretensions within what he gradually learns is his society's version of reality and to become himself within the roles and techniques at his disposal. No wonder, then, that man's play takes place on the border of dangerous alternatives and is always beset both with burdening conflicts and with liberating choices.

At the same time, however, human play as well as adult

ritualizations and rituals seem to serve the function of adaptation to the "pseudo" aspects of human "reality": for, as I will point out in some detail later, man, in addition to making gigantic strides in learning to know nature and the uses it can be put to, has yet also striven to maintain prejudged assumptions concerning the ordained excellence of particular versions of man. Thus, his playful imagination does not only serve all that is and could be, it also is forced to endow that which, so he is clearly taught, must be if he is to be judged sane and worthy. Youthful rebellion always attempts to create new leeway for new and potential roles in such assumed realities; but the very condition of pseudospeciation has made man's playfulness a matter both of freedom and of bondage, both of enhanced life and of multiplied death.

I have attempted to illustrate the way in which youthful play-acting and the assumption or usurpation of historical roles can border on each other. But we must now account for the fact that new ritualizations are, indeed, apt to miscarry because of the "horrible fact that the hate which the young bear us is tribal hate." And, indeed, it seems that the shift in the overall ecological and technological conditions of mankind has led, at least within the orbit of the American industrial world culture (which includes the World War II enemies of the United States), to a new grouping of pseudospecies: on one side all the young people across the borders of former empires and on the other the whole "old" generation.

It is obvious enough that the young reject, above all, the insignia and the attitudes which have marked their victimization and heroification as soldiers serving one of the pseudospecies extant now. Because they carry this protest literally on the sleeve, we can now add to the subjects to be reviewed the ritual importance of human *display*, for we are reminded of the prominence, in all of classical warfare, of the resplendent uniforms, topped by animal plumage, which was intended to unite and divide the young men of the world into warriors serving either the right and godly or the wrong and evil species: that the display of physical insignia signifying human pseudospeciation imitate those of animal speciation is only too obvious. And it begin to make sense that the rebellious youth of today is displaying, instead, an impressive array of self-contradicting insignia, often mocking all uniformity by mixing fragments of military uniforms (and even of flags) with the ornaments of relaxed brotherhood. For youth attempts to create not only new arenas for involvements and commitments, but also such new types of heroes as are essential to the emergence of a whole "human being" representative of mankind itself—if and when the old have abrogated their pseudospecies, or have been destroyed. In the meantime, youth often seems to feel that it can enforce basic changes only by mockingly insisting on a moratorium without end and an unlimited arena of its own, and it is often only with drugs that they can aver the remaining boundaries and simulate a free territory within. This is a state of affairs open to all kinds of group retrogressions as well as personal regressions.* But, then, adolescent regressions always have been, to some extent, semideliberate recapitulations of childhood fantasy serving the adaptive purpose of reviving what infantile playfulness was sacrificed to the established order for use on new ideological

---

* In a paper on dissent, I have offered a topology of such semideliberate retrogression, relating them to the stages of life and thus indicating both their potentially prophetic and their potentially dangerous significance for the individuals involved (10).

frontiers. Similarly, large-scale historical retrogressions often seem to be semideliberate attempts to invoke the revolutions of the past in the name of a future revolution as yet neither defined nor localized nor fixed in time. But the extremes noted here may be necessary aspects of a shift, the outcome of which can only be appraised when it will be clear where such playful trends combine with the discipline and the competence necessary for sustained change.

If one accepts the theory of a shift from the pseudospecies mentality to an all-human one (and this is the hopeful aspect on which Konrad Lorenz and I would agree), one may well see in the radical display of youth an upheaval necessary for an elemental regrouping which transvaluates past ideals of excellence and heroism in the service of a more universal speciation. To be sure, much horrible hate and much resultant paralysis is thus transferred to the intergenerational struggle where it appears to be hopelessly raw and untrained in comparison to the age-old stance and stamina of uniformed and disciplined military behavior. This probably is the cause of occasional enactments of totally "senseless" cruelty and of dramatic murder for the sake of a vindictive illusion of extinguishing the established.

But we may well remind ourselves of two momentous developments characteristic of the other, the adult side of playing history. The first is the fact that adult man, with the help of the most creative expansion of scientific and organizational leeway (remember Einstein's playfulness), has created a world technically ready to eliminate mankind in one instant for the sake of one nation or another that cannot stop playing empire. Is it any wonder that some of the most romantic and the most destructive behavior in modern youth seems to mock us by anticipating the day when the nuclear holocaust *has* occurred?

The second fact is the disintegration of paternalistic dominance, both in familiar relations and in the "minds of man." For this again we blame primarily the antipaternal attitude of the young. Following Freud we have obediently persisted in referring to the origins of the rebellious complex in childhood as the Oedipus Complex. But (as Dr. Piers has also pointed out in these symposia) we have thus immortalized as inescapable only the behavior of the son Oedipus, who unknowingly slew his father as the Oracle had predicted, while we have paid little attention to the fact that this father had such faith in the Oracle's opaque announcement and in his own interpretation of it, that he was willing to dispose of his son. But maybe Laius did only more openly and more dramatically what may be implicit in circumcisions, puberty rites, and "confirmations" of many kinds. As a prize for certified adulthood, the fathers all limit and forestall some frightening potentialities of development dangerous to "the system." And they all strive to appropriate the new individual for the pseudospecies, marking and branding him as potentially dangerous, initiating him into the prescribed limits of activities, inducting him into a preferred service, and preparing him for being sacrificed in holy wars. Maybe they only underscore ritually what human development and the structure of human society accomplish anyway. For after having played at a variety of choices, most adults submit to so-called reality, that is, a consolidation of established facts, of acquired methods, of defined roles, and of overweening values. Such consolidation is deemed necessary not only for a style of acting and interacting, but, above all, for the bringing up of the next generation of children. They, it is hoped, will, from their childhood play and their juvenile role experimentation, move right into the dominant means of production and will invest their playfulness and their search for identity in the daily necessity to work for the higher glory of the pseudospecies.

Today, Laius and Oedipus face one another in a different confrontation. For even as the youth of divergent countries begin to look, talk, and feel alike—and this whether they are rebelling against industrial civilization or are, in fact, rapidly learning the prerequisite skills—so does the older generation appear to become more and more alike and stereotyped. For they impersonate a new and universal type, the efficient member of an organized occupation or a profession, playing free and equal while being at the mercy of mass-produced roles, of standardized consumership, and of rampant bureaucratization. But all these are developments which, in fact, take the play out of work—and this not (or not only) because of a Calvinistic choice to separate the two for the sake of righteousness, but because it can't be helped. And this seems to be the message of much of the mockery of the young, that if there must be defined roles, it may be better to go on playing at choosing them, than to become their ready puppets.

IX

A concluding section on play in adulthood can only be an opening section for another, a future essay. For here we enter both the twilight of what is called "reality" and the ambiguities of the word *play*—and these two assuredly are related to each other. Even as man protests the pure truth just because he is the animal who can lie—and pretend to be natural—so he strives to be in tune with hard reality just because he so easily falls for illusions and abstractions. And both truth and reality are at issue when man must define what he means when he says he is playing—or not playing.

The poet has it, that man is never more human than when he plays. But what must he do and be, and in what context, to be both adult and playful: must he do something in which he feels again as if he were a playing child, or a youth in a game? Must he step outside of his most serious and most fateful concerns? Or must he transcend his everyday condition and be "beside himself" in fantasy, ecstasy, or "togetherness"?

Maybe an epigenetic view makes it unnecessary to categorize so sharply. The adult once was a child and a youth. He will never be either again: but neither will he ever be without the heritage of those former states. In fact, I would postulate that, in order to be truly adult, he must on each level renew some of the playfulness of childhood and some of the sportiveness of the young. As we have seen, the child in his play and games as well as the young person in his pranks and sports and forays into politics, protected as they both are, up to a point, from having their play-acting "count" as irreversible action, nevertheless are dealing with central concerns both of settling the past and of anticipating the future. So must the adult, beyond playful and sportive activities specified as such, remain playful in the center of his concerns and concerned with opportunities to renew and increase the leeway and scope of his and his fellow man's activities. Whatever the precursors of a specifically adult playfulness, it must grow with and through the adult stages even as these stages can come about only by such renewal. But here we are faced with a threefold dilemma: the adult's marked inner separation (re-

pression and all) from much of his childhood; the limitations
of adolescent identity development in terms of available roles;
and a certain intrinsic intolerance in adult institutions to the
renewal of the identity crisis. Adult institutions want to ban
the turmoil of youth even as they want to banish the thought
of decline and death. This leaves adulthood in a position of
double defensiveness and with a need to bolster the boundaries
of what to a given generation of adults seems "real."

"Creative" people know this, and the poet Frost said it. In
an encounter with two tramps who see him chopping away at
some wood and remind him of the fateful division of work
and play, he intones:

> But yield who will to their separation
> My object in living is to unite
> My avocation and my vocation
> As my two eyes make one in sight.
> Only where love and need are one,
> And the play is work for mortal stakes,
> Is the deed ever really done
> For heaven and the future's sakes. (11)

We may for the moment ignore the fact that the men thus
addressed were looking for work; we know that one man's
play and work may be another's unemployment. But taking
Frost's creativity as a measure, we may add to his formulation the postulate that the adult, in combining vocation and
avocation, creates leeway for himself while creating leeway
for those within his scope of mutuality.

At the beginning of this essay, I compared a child's solitary
play construction with the function of a dramatic performance in adulthood: in both, a theme and a conflict, dominant
in the "big" world, are meaningfully condensed into a micro-

sphere and into a spectacle and a speculum, a mirror of inner and outer conditions. (The stage play is a tragedy, where a representative person is shown as one who can envisage greater freedom for his time and age but finds that he has forfeited it for lack of inner and outer *Spielraum*.) The dimly lit theater thus deals with the reflection an individual fate of all those areas of public action which occur in "all the world," in the light of day. But if man, as pointed out, calls these spheres "theaters," "spectacles," and "scenarios" one wonders sometimes which is metaphorical for what. For man endows such spheres of highest reality, too, with a ceremonial and procedural aura which permits him to get engaged with a certain abandon, with intensified loyalty, and often with increased energy and efficiency, but also with a definite sacrifice of plain good judgment. Some of these special spheres are endowed with rituals in super-real halls, be they cathedrals, courts, or castles. But their hypnotic power as a visionary sphere transcends all locality and institutionalization: we may think here of the monarchy or the presidency, of the law courts or the seats of government: all these, while denoting an obligation of superhuman excellence, are also apt to cover, with everybody's connivance, a multitude of contradictions and pretenses accepted as the "rules of the game." Any observing visitor to a legislative chamber or a chief executive's mansion will not escape an occasional eerie sense of unreality in such factories of decision which must determine irreversible shifts in what will seem compellingly real to so many, and in what to generations to come will seem worth living, dying, and killing for—remember the Iron Curtain! Most fateful for mankind as a species (we cannot say this too often) is the tendency to redivide the political scene in such a way that those "on the other side" suddenly appear to be changed in quality, reduced to statistical items and worthy only of "body counts." However, the aura of some (if not all) of these spheres is being diminished in our very time by the production through the media of new spheres of vision, with their strange interplay of service, truth, and business. Some such spheres, as the "national scene," or the "forum of public opinion," or the "arena of politics" are also being studied in their major dimensions by social science: but we know as yet little about their dynamic influences on personality, on identity, and, indeed, on sanity— either in individuals or in cliques, in organized groups or in the masses. The fact is that such phenomena, in turn, can only be studied by "fields" of approach and "schools" of thought and by theoretical systems which themselves fascinate by their ability to organize appearances and to make visible the factual truth. But science, at least, perseveres in an in-built critique of science itself as well as of the scientist; and this in terms increasingly accessible to all "species" of men. If factuality is the soul of all search for reality, then mankind is on the way to agreeing to a joint reality; and if truth can only emerge from an all-human actuality, all men may, someday soon, be "in touch" with each other.

I am suggesting for a future occasion, then, that we take a new good look not only at those occasions when adults claim that they are playing like children, or play-acting on the legitimate stage, but also such other occasions when they insist with deadly righteousness that they are playing for "real" stakes and yet, sooner or later, appear to have been role-playing puppets in imaginary spheres of "necessity."

If at the beginning of this paper I made a "leap" from play construction to theater, let me now make one back from adult reality to infancy. Could it not be that all these spheres have a place in adult man's life equivalent to that visual sphere which in the very first year of life provides, all at once, an integrated sensory universe, a mutuality with a maternal person, and a beginning of inner order, and thus provides the basic leeway for growth, action, and interaction? I do not wish to overdo this: in adulthood such visualized spheres obviously overlap with concrete areas of established power and organized technique which have their own rationale of continuity and growth. Yet they all share in that quality of vision which not only renders experience vastly more comprehendable, but also provides man with collective and individual affirmations of an emotional kind. And, indeed, the vision is often attended to by some kind of goddess (made visible as Nike in graceful flight, or Freedom baring her breast to the storm of revolution, "blind" Justice, or somber and selfless Truth, not to speak of "smiling" Success) which, indeed, gives recognition in turn for having been recognized. These visions, it must be repeated, can bring out the best in man as they encourage, with a greater leeway, courage and solidarity, imagination and invention. The human tragedy has been and is that the highest of these goddesses are overshadowed by the demands of the pseudospecies, which eventually employs even the most heroic deeds and the most sincere gains in knowledge, for the exploitation and enslavement, the denigration and annihilation, or, at any rate, the checkmating of other "kinds" of men. As any visual order must always discriminate as well as abstract, it is hard for man not to make himself more real and his world more comprehensible without envisaging others as expendable or nonexistent— even eight hundred million Chinese behind a bamboo curtain.

X

And then, there are the great adults who are adult and are called great precisely because their sense of identity vastly surpasses the roles foisted upon them, their vision opens up new realities, and their gift of communication revitalizes actuality. In freeing themselves from rigidities and inhibitions they create new freedoms for some oppressed categories of men, find a new leeway for suppressed energies, and give new scope to followers who, in turn, feel more adult for being sanctioned and encouraged. The great, we say, are "gifted" with genius; but, of course, they often must destroy, too, and will seem evil to those whom they endanger, or whom they exclude.

Freud, in freeing the neurotics of his repressed era from the onus of degeneracy, invented a method of playful communication called "free association" which has taught man (way beyond the clinical setting) to play back and forth between what is most conscious to him and what has remained unverbalized or become repressed. And he has taught man to give freer play to fantasies and impulses which, if not realized in sexual foreplay or "sublimated" in actuality, help only to narrow his *Spielraum* to the point of explosions in symptomatic actions.

But as Freud "took morality for granted," he also treated adulthood and reality as matters on which all enlightened man would agree. Yet, I think, he made the point that only when man has faced his neurotic isolation and stagnation is he free to let his imagination and his sense of truth come up against the existential dilemmas which transcend passing realities.

Marx, it is interesting to recall, spoke of a *coming* adulthood

of the species. At the celebration of Marx's 150th birthday in
Trier, Robert Tucker pointed out that "self-realization, or becoming fully human, was not for Marx a problem that an
individual person could solve on his own. It could only be
solved within the framework of the self-realization of the
species at the end of history." (12) Marx referred to history
both as an *Entfremdungsgeschichte* that made of man an
alienated creature, and as a *growth process of the human race*,
an *Entstehungsakt:* only a kind of rebirth could overcome the
submersion of the aesthetic production "according to the laws
of beauty" and the deadening of all playfulness by unfree
labor. Tucker suggested that we may today well be in a final
"maturation crisis." "If so," he added, "the most serious aspect
of the crisis is the . . . tendency of most people and even the
leaders of nations to assume that no great change is called for,
that we immature humans are already grown up."

Now, a few years later, it is obvious, that this awareness,
while maybe not yet accessible to "most people" and their
leaders, has spread at least to the point where the young people
deny that the older ones have grown up. In fact, there is a
pervasive suspicion of the whole idea of growing up; and there
is also an increased awareness of history, which among other
things teaches that the revolutionary leeway gained yesterday
can become the obsession and the suppression of today, and
this for reasons immanent in greatness itself as well as in adulthood itself. If great men inspire vast changes with a creative
playfulness both driven and (necessarily) destructive, their
followers must consolidate change, which means to take the
risk out of it. Neither the task of a Marxian critique of unconscious "historical" motivation, nor the Freudian one of an
inner enslavement to the immaturity both of impulse and of

conscience can be said to be accomplished in any foreseeable future.

But the method of yesterday can also become part of a wider consciousness today. Psychoanalysis can go about defining its own place in history and yet continue to observe its traditional subject matter, namely the symptoms of repressions and suppressions—including their denial. It can study successive re-repressions in relation to historical change: there can be little doubt but that our enlightened age has set out to prove Freud wrong by doing openly and with a vengeance what he said were secret desires, warded off by inhibitions. We can learn to find out how we have contributed to such developments by our exclusive reliance (also culturally and historically determined) on the "dominance of the intellect" which often made the acceptance of psychoanalytic theory and vocabulary the measure of a man's adaptation. We know now (and the study of play confirms us in this) that the comprehension of Freud's *Wirklichkeit* must go beyond one of its meanings, namely reality, and include that of actuality. (13) For if reality is the structure of facts consensually agreed upon in a given stage of knowledge, actuality is the leeway created by new forms of interplay. Without actuality, reality becomes a prison of stereotypy, while actuality always must retest reality to remain truly playful. To fully understand this we must study for each stage of life the interpenetration of the cognitive and the affective as well as the moral and the instinctual. We may then realize that in adulthood an individual gains leeway for himself, as he creates it for others: here is the soul of adult play.

In conclusion, we must take note of another "gap" in our civilization which only partly coincides with the generational one. It is that between a grim determination to play out established and divisive roles, functions, and competencies to their bitter ends; and, on the other hand, new kinds of group life characterized by a total playfulness, which simulates vast imagination (often drug-induced), sexual and sensual freedom, and a verbal openness often way beyond the integrative means of individuals, not to speak of technological and economic realities. In the first area, that of habituated pragmatism, leading individuals make a grim effort at pretending that they are in full command of the facts and by no means role-playing—a claim which in fact gives them a vanishing credibility. The playful crowd, on the other hand, often seems to play all too hard at playing and at pretending that they are already sharing a common humanity, by-passing those technical and political developments which must provide the material basis for "one world." But man is a tricky animal; and adults playing all too hard at role-playing or at simulating naturalness, honesty, and intimacy may end up being everybody and yet nobody, in touch with all and yet not close to anybody.

Yet, there are also signs that man may indeed be getting ready to renounce his claims on the ancient prerogatives of special pseudospecies, such as the abuse of others and the waste of resources in the environment and in inner life. Psychoanalysis, at this juncture, must remain vigilant in regard to the anxieties and rages aroused where a wider identity will endanger existing styles of instinctuality and identity and traditional visions of morality and reality.

But we must always also be receptive to new forms of interplay; and we must always come back to the children and learn to recognize the signs of unknown resources which might yet flourish in the vision of one mankind on one earth and its outer reaches.

REFERENCES

1. Erik H. Erikson, *Childhood and Society*, 2nd ed. (New York: W. W. Norton, 1963).

2. In *The Man-Made Object*, ed. Gyorgy Kepes (New York: Braziller, 1966).

3. Ascanio Condivi, *Vita di Michelangiolo Buonarotti* (Rome, 1553). Here translated by Alice Wohl.

4. Charles Seymour, *Michelangelo's David: A Search for Identity* (Pittsburgh: University of Pittsburgh, 1967), p. 7.

5. 1 Corinthians 13:12.

6. Creighton Gilbert, *Complete Poems and Selected Letters of Michelangelo* (New York: McGraw-Hill, 1965), p. 5.

7. Jacques Hadamard, *The Psychology of Invention in the Mathematical Field* (Princeton: Princeton University, 1945), pp. 142–43.

8. Quoted in Holton, "On Trying to Understand Scientific Genius," *The American Scholar* 41, no. 1 (Winter 1971/72).

9. "A Discussion of Ritualisation of Behavior in Animals and Man," organized by Sir Julian Huxley, F.R.S., *Philosophical Transactions of the Royal Society of London*, Series B, no. 772, vol. 251, pp. 337–49.

10. "Reflections on the Dissent of Contemporary Youth," *International Journal of Psychoanalysis* 51, 11, 1970.

11. Robert Frost, "Two Tramps in Mud-Time."

12. Robert Tucker, *The Marxian Revolutionary Idea* (New York: W. W. Norton, 1969), p. 215.

13. Erik H. Erikson, *Insight and Responsibility* (New York: W. W. Norton, 1964), chap. 5.

Epilogue

A by-product of the knowledge explosion is a greater and greater distance between the researcher who deals with high level abstractions and the practitioner in any given field. This distance is in many instances being bridged by a chain of people with interlocking or mutually enhancing competences; people who pass on downward and translate and apply research findings or else pass on practical experience upward for further testing and refinement. It is by such relay that the nuclear scientist becomes pertinent to the work of the nurse's aid and the attendant at the filling station, or the economist to the man at the cash register, and so on.

One of the most notable exceptions to this is the field of child care. Its relay system is almost nonexistent. In vast areas of Western civilization child care and early education are in fact completely disconnected from the disciplines relevant to what one might define as the tasks of all education: *survival, competence, enjoyment of life*. It is as if medicine, psychology, the social sciences had nothing pertinent to offer.

One can't help speculating on the factors that brought about this schizophrenic state of affairs. Why is it that legislators as well as school boards are so often unaware of successive cognitive steps: The subtle communications between mother and infant, communications which make the difference between a truly human existence and merely vegetating? Why is it that the connection between play and higher math escapes us? Or the connection between a child's rage and anxiety on the one hand and his attention span on the other? Or the mutual influence between a ten-year-old boy and the neighborhood he lives in? Or the mutual (yes, mutual) need between the aged and little children?

One reason that comes to mind is that applying scientific findings frequently sounds easier than it proves to be; that there is no formula whereby a family of seven can be treated three times a day to five mgs. of Piaget, no absolutely "responsive environment" to make every child respond. This, of course, does not mean that a classroom cannot be conducive to learning, but merely that it is not equally conducive to children of all ages, both sexes, and regardless of their economic background and cultural heritage. To expect that any practical or even vaguely similar results in children is at worst an Orwellian thought, and at best simplistic. It is an expectation which could only have occurred in an age of mass production and standardization, when people are in fact often viewed as mechanical gadgets. There are very likely historical reasons for the Big Gap. Perhaps education's direct descent from religion, specifically the derivation of schools in Western civilization from monastic orders, might have brought it under the sway of dogma, rather than rational thought. This historic development differs in essence from the development of the natural sciences, which seems to have taken place largely in opposition to organized religion rather than because of it.

Our reluctance to apply the results of research to child care may, however, be due to a third reason, an intrapsychic one. Children are not only the prime objects of our highest hopes but also prime subjects of our intensive anger. All children are, by definition, at times cumbersome, expensive, and ungrateful. Worse yet, they seem to mirror those aspects which we disliked most in ourselves and hoped to have overcome: our irrationality, our murderous inclinations, our lasting preoccupations with the small sensual pleasures of our childhood.

Because of our high hopes for our children we build child care centers, schools, clinics, universities. Because of our hostility we perhaps deny them the best of our cultural heritage; for instance, the practical consequences of scientific findings about man. If, however, we must warn against the simplistic application of these findings what then does developmental psychology have to offer to child care? Some of the main contributions are negative: what is to be avoided or feared or used sparingly; which factors are within the spectrum of growth-promoting practices in a given culture, which ones are outside. As E. H. Erikson put it, "While it is quite clear what *must* happen to keep the baby alive—the minimum supply necessary, and and what *must not* happen lest he be physically damaged or chronically upset—there is a certain leeway in regard to what *may* happen, and different cultures make extensive use of the prerogative to decide what they consider workable and insist on calling it necessary." It is a signal function of this book to contribute to the clarification of universal musts and must nots and to the colorful spectrum of the mays.

Among the lines of thought coming out of Peter Wolff's paper, there are two of great importance for the practitioner. One is obviously this: If cognition can be achieved by disadvantaged children via alternate pathways, then we must not only find out what they are, but also how to facilitate, if possible, their pursuit. The other one, related to the first, concerns healthy normal children. We tend to talk about them as if they were a definable category, when in fact we know that there is no norm. Rather, there is a huge variety of personalities whose social, emotional, cognitive development takes place in sequential steps within given (critical) periods, apropos of a problem that suddenly seems to present itself, or a intrapersonal or inner conflict that must somehow be resolved. Each human being approaches these hurdles at different times in his life with different affects ranging from mildly interested to eager and lusty to grimly, almost desperate. We are perhaps too prone to attribute the strength of the affect and the conflict to environmental conditions. The idea of alternate pathways suggests that one particular child living under conditions of outward duress finds them more readily than do others. He is, as it were, more gifted in replacing *one* mode of "getting there" with another one. We must then allow for the possibility that such relative importance or unimportance to the point of skipping expected sequences also exists in children growing up in a favorable environment. Therein lies a warning for educators. For once educators accept a developmental theory they are often prone to turn it into a dogma. Such was the fate of concepts like the Oedipal phase, operational thinking, the juxtaposition of trust-mistrust, or the ubiquity of adolescent hostility and talent. The possibility of alternate pathways for poverty as well as middle-class children is an antidote to educational dogmatism.

The book's most frequent and most powerful theme is play. Play is a Must of the first order for individuals (Piaget, Spitz, Murphy) and for mankind (Lorenz, Erikson). This main theme leads to a number of imperatives for the practitioner, but also raises some questions of awe-inspiring magnitude. If, for instance, children must (playfully) re-invent in order to

understand logical and mathematical principles, then it becomes necessary that every public school that does not want
to defeat its very purpose give every child a measure of freedom to explore, while protecting him from a barrage of dis-
tracting stimuli, including excessive fear and rage. On behalf
of optimal academic learning we would then have to insist on
a measure of privacy and benign order for every classroom
and all places where children—indeed people of all ages—are
expected to think, fantasize, and play. Here, however, we must
pause and ask ourselves how our advocacy jibes with two
phenomena. One is the behavior frequently observed in the
present generation of adolescents, who create their leeway
(inner arena) for what seems like play by voluntarily submitting to a veritable onslaught of stimuli, achieved with the
help of rock bands, strobe lights, and drugs. The result is a
kind of privacy, with fantasies and often a lessening of interpersonal idiosyncrasies.

The other phenomenon is equally puzzling to the older generation: The conscientious middle-class student who does his
homework in front of the glaring, blaring TV set, the very
antithesis of seclusion. Perhaps the answer lies in a sharper
differentiation between inner play experiences, with the focus
on the two elements stressed by Erikson, freedom and limits.
The "trip" seems to be all freedom (often frighteningly so)
and devoid of all disciplined active mastery. "Trips" may ultimately spark artistic creations (which by definition involves
craftsmanship and deliberation) but not while they last. Only
when a degree of sobriety has been regained. The pupil in
front of the screen, on the other hand, seems to be combating
the intolerable boredom of a routine assignment which may
give him more than the necessary confines needed for active
mastery, but no choice about the what and how. The TV

pupil is the polar opposite of the "tripper." Neither one has *both* ingredients for productive play at his disposal. If, however, problem-solving play is contingent on both leeway and limits, and if we take such play as seriously as it deserves to be taken, that means that all institutionalized child care and education must beware of either anarchy or regimentation. It means that children need teachers with self-discipline but without too many constrictions. Above all else, in order to avoid the prisonlike character or the frightening laissez faire of such institutions there must be a ratio of responsible adults appropriate to the developmental stages of the children.

But what about the preliminaries to play, the months of fundamental education and beginning mutuality? Here we are on much safer ground. Differences between human beings in accordance with their cultural matrix and their chance fate become stronger and cumulative as they grow older. But infants are very much alike, and their needs are almost identical. We can, therefore, state some universal prerequisites for growth promoting play and for optimal growth—with no guarantee for success, of course. If, however, we do the best we can, and do it to the best of our knowledge, then we must see to it that every infant has *one* mother. The gamut of sensory percepts, increasingly lustful and fused into a whole by vision, requires that a mother, the *same* mother, take care of him. Not an array of figures, however benevolent or knowledgeable. Her presence is necessary for the growing distinction between the "I" and the "You," for the number of repeatedly practiced skills basic to all further learning, and above all for that sense of well-being and wholeness which makes later schisms bearable or even constructive, renders later differently structured interrelationships possible, and ultimately can lead to a sense of a meaningful and rounded life in old age. The practical must not refer here to such institutions as foster placement, or impersonal institutional care. Foster-placing young children, if and where it cannot be avoided, must carry with it a virtual guarantee for a long duration, if not for the entire childhood and adolescence. A transition to another group of people with whom he is to establish relationships, such a transition must not happen abruptly, but so that the child has a chance to grope his way into a new set of rules and rituals before he relinquishes his old ones. The Foster-child Syndrome could, in fact, be defined by the forever tentative nature of interplay with adult partners. The child mistakenly assumes that the rules of the game (what goes and what does not) are the same in family number two as they were in family number one. The assumption usually proves incorrect, and the child then is forced to recognize a new set of rights and wrongs and to more or less abide by these new rules until he is placed into a different home. There the guessing game starts again. Interplay of short duration renders a child unable to make the rules his own, to really internalize them. The victims of having too many families are known for their frequent moral deficits and do not achieve relative solidification which under better circumstances permits the young person to become an adult. What, we now must ask, constitutes "better circumstances"? It can be stated, but it cannot be so easily prescribed. For as human beings get older the Musts and Must Nots are less and less related to education and increasingly contingent on the broad social scene. The relative solidification of a personal identity depends on an "ideological universe," sufficiently defined, yet flexible enough so a young person "can anchor his readiness for loyalty in social reality."

To achieve this social reality many things must happen. The

current discrepancy between the games of the young people, self-contradictory and farcical as they seem, but deadly earnest in their search for "new arenas . . . and new types of heroes" and the inherently contradictory games old people play, this discrepancy must be narrowed. For even though they profess to love their sons it is "the old men who make war," and it is the "young men who die in it" (Dalton Trumbo). What are the approaches that must be taken by both sides to bridge the discrepancy? For the young people, it entails the acceptance of the limited arena, and perhaps the acceptance of the fact that compromises are inevitable. Their task is comparatively easy, for it comes to many quite naturally with (literally or figuratively) becoming a parent. For the old people the task is colossal. For it means insight into their own and every human being's destructive potential and the abandoning of personal attachments to obsolete rituals in favor of new ones which they can share with their children. It means to find new applications for technical achievements, applications that serve the survival, not of some subspecies, but of the whole human race.

Even so, Erikson makes us feel that we, however guardedly, may be hopeful. For we have scientific and hence objective tools at our disposal, which may yet enable human beings to see their problems in a similar manner and agree on a "joint reality." To be practical once more, the road to this future, if it is not to be a mere utopia, that road is stony and begins with introspection.

Maria W. Piers